BARBELLA

Copyright ©2016 Lane Rockford Orsak

All rights reserved. Except as permitted under the U.S. Copyright Act of 1976, no part of this publication may be reproduced, distributed, or transmitted in any form or by any means, or stored in a database or retrieval system, without the prior permission of the author.

This is a work of fiction. All incidents and dialogue, and all the characters with the exception of some well-known historical figures, are products of the author's imagination and are not to be construed as real. Where real-life historical figures and public figures appear, the situations, incidents, and dialogues concerning those persons are entirely fictional and are not intended to depict actual events or to change the entirely fictional nature of the work. In all other respects, any resemblance to persons living or dead is entirely coincidental.

First Edition: May 2016
Lulu Author. All rights reserved.
www.lulu.com

ISBN: 978-1-365-04751-0

Book design by Michael Campbell, MCWriting.com

For more information visit www.laneorsak.com

BARBELLA

A NOVEL BY

LANE ROCKFORD ORSAK

Also by Lane Rockford Orsak:

Keiko the Fairy: The Kujiki
Keiko the Fairy: The Silk Road
Keiko the Fairy: Yonaguni

Clown White

Contents

One

   Miss Palmer's School,
      Farmington, Connecticut 3

   The Spark 9

   Reconciliation 15

   Senior Year 23

   Banging the Piano 29

   Prelude in C Minor 35

   The Sting 41

   The Requiem 49

Two

   The Boardwalk 57

   Gold's 61

   Parkour 69

   Maxi Ho 73

   The Ho Down 79

   Home Sweet Home 93

   The Gang 97

   Apti-mistic 105

   Trouble in Dogtown 111

   Ho Gym 123

Three

- *Snapshot: Two Months Later* 129
- *To Franco With Love* 137
- *In The Light of Day* 155

Four

- *The Guy In the White Hat* 167
- *The Jail Bird Song* 173
- *The RoosterCock* 177
- *The Radiant Child* 187

Five

- *Nine Months Later* 203
- *The Fine Line* 207
- *Overcoming Coming* 213
- *Old Man and The Sea* 215
- *Maxi Ho Gym on Steroids* 221
- *Full Circle* 231
- *Strong Enough To Be My Man* 235
- *Epilogue* 239

About the author 243

Special thanks to:
Gia Innes-Bell for inspiration,
her mother for appearing on the cover
of Muscle & Fitness magazine,
her muscle-amazing father,
Gambit the Chechen Parkour wizard,
all the trainers at the Hills Fitness Center,
the Starbucks Gang,
and to my lovely wife for her love and support.

· · · · · · · · · · · · · · · · · ·

One

Miss Palmer's School, Farmington, Connecticut

• • • • • • • • • • • • •

IT ALL STARTED the night my unstoppably charming and inquisitive English roommate, Clarissa Westwick, walked in and overheard me congratulate Mom about her upcoming appearance in *Muscle & Fitness* magazine.

When I finished the call, Clarissa couldn't wait to pounce, but held decorum by lightly inquiring, "Bar Darling, what's all this about your mum in a magazine? Why is she featured? Some kind of society rubbish?"

It was a secret, and one I meant to keep. I don't know if it was because she recently transferred to Miss Palmer's School mid-term from a boarding school in England and might feel as isolated and lonely as I did, or if I was simply tired of covering up my identity to avoid getting blasted by these East Coast secret-society bitches.

Whatever the reason, I just turned toward Clarissa and spilled it.

"My mother is a body-sculpting model."

Clarissa appeared utterly gobsmacked, as if her fine leather shoe had just unexpectedly stuck to a thick wad of chewing gum. She stared off into the distance and muttered, "So, Bar Darling, does that mean that your mother is a porn star?"

"No, Clarissa, it means that my mother is a body-builder and will be featured on the upcoming cover of *Muscle & Fitness* magazine."

"Right darling. Why don't you bring out your massive stash of candy from under your bed and I'll make us a lovely pot of tea, with a wee dash of whiskey, and we can have a proper chin wag!" Clarissa said with a seductive smile.

"Jolly good," I replied, without realizing how ridiculous I sounded.

It was as if the floodgates had opened. Overriding my usual self-loathing thoughts was the greater exhilaration of finally having *someone* I felt I could talk with—honestly—at school. Clarissa seemed so excited and asked me endless amounts of questions. I showed her gobs of bodybuilding photos of my muscle-amazing mom. And accidentally included another portrait.

"Right, so Bar Darling, who is the Italian stallion? My God, I'd like to play pony with this one!"

"Well, that one is my dad!"

Clarissa's eyes widened as if I had just told her that I was *doing* Prince Harry, who was her third cousin.

"Bar Darling, are you telling me that both of your parents are professional bodybuilders?"

"Well, technically, my mother never used steroids, and she doesn't compete. But my father was a serious professional competitor."

Clarissa paused and stared at me for the longest time with her big, sensual blue eyes. "So where did all of this take place?"

"We lived in Venice Beach, California. I was practically raised in Gold's Gym."

I began to feel sick to my stomach breaking my own rule of *never* telling anyone the truth about my parents back home, knowing full well that if anyone found out it would be a social earthquake—a true ten on the Richter scale.

"Clarissa, I *really like you* and I want to share everything with you, but you have to promise me that this will stay between us—absolutely *no one* can know about this. Can you promise me?"

"Of course darling, you don't think I am that duplicitously daft do you?"

"Of course not." I said, hoping my instincts were right.

"So darling, let us begin with the obvious question, how in God's name did you select Miss Palmer's School?" Clarissa seemed to never ask what she really meant, which was *How in God's name can your parents afford this place?* At first, I thought I would offer the more socially acceptable response about the educational trust fund that Grandma Pippa left for me. But the real reason I was here was my Dad's accusation.

Clarissa gave a polite giggle to bring me back to the conversation. "Have you gone mental? It would appear the sheer anguish and pressure associated with Head Master Wescott's speech today at assembly about the virtues associated with living a life rooted in honesty, all that business about how we would, in fact, receive an education *beyond the norm,* and all that rot has rendered you incapable of speech."

I laughed nervously and suggested that my life was so tiresome it might keep us up too late, and besides, didn't she have an English exam in the morning?

"Darling, do you really think that this prissy little *American* girl's school can teach me how to speak English?" It was her way of saying, *If you think that I am going to let you get away with not telling me the truth about why you are here—you are mad!* I popped a small handful of candy corns and drank some more whiskey-stained tea and decided to finally just take a chance and tell her.

"I've never really been good at talking about my life and it has been such a long time since I was living back home. Bear with me…"

"Take your time, darling," Clarissa purred, pouring more whiskey and tea.

Just as I found the emotional strength to begin, the dorm room door swung open as if to say *Ah ha, I caught ya!* Standing in the doorway, wearing a man's red plaid flannel robe with her short brown hair heavily parted, with one pink curler on her bangs, was our House Director, Miss Porter, aka "Pete." She gave us a stern look.

"Ladies, I'm sure that you have a compelling reason for being awake past curfew, but if you are not in bed and asleep in the next five minutes, you will both be reporting to Miss Wescott's office in the morning."

I'm not sure if Clarissa was more horrified by Miss Porter's appearance or the fact that we were drinking whiskey in our room—let alone after lights-out, a punishment that could lead to immediate expulsion—but it caused her to spray tea all over me, through her nostrils, and scream with extinguished laughter.

Pete snapped, "Miss Clarissa, if you can't find your equilibrium in this room, perhaps you will sleep better on my sofa bed…"

"That won't be necessary, Miss Porter. I'm sure that Bar Darling and I are exhausted from studying and will go to bed with haste."

Pete shut the door snugly, and we slammed our faces into our pillows, screaming with laughter.

"My God, at first, I thought Pete was Mr. Wiggins coming round for a romp on the desk!" Clarissa was referring to the latest big sex scandal at Miss Palmer's School involving Coach Wiggins, our resident predator in perpetual warm up pants. We both choked with laughter, repeating, "Oh, Coach Wiggins, can you help me try this on?"

Recently, Coach Wiggins was discovered by his wife, a counselor at our school, in his office with a day student, Trisha Turner. Trisha was atop his desk with her tiny green track shorts around her ankles and Coach Wiggins's stretchy pants around his. Word had it that Mrs. Wiggins walked in and screamed, "Will Wiggins, what are you doing?" In the insanity of the moment, he responded wryly, "Oh, we are just trying on our new track uniforms for the big game on Saturday!"

Clarissa smirked. "Did you pick up on old Pete's invitation for one of her famous 'sleepovers'?"

We both buried our faces again into our pillows, laughing hysterically. Last year, Pete was having "sleepovers" with one of the older girls named Becca. When Pete told her she loved her and wanted to leave Miss Palmer's and live together, Becca freaked out and confided in her roommate Claire Fitzhugh... who confided in and told Joan Thomeson, who confided in Jane Wilkinson, who confided in Bunny Perkins, who I overheard tell someone seated next to me in Comparative Lit class, "Becca is moving to New York City to marry Pete. Becca is going to be a firefighter and Pete wants to act on Broadway."

Something you learn fairly soon after arriving at Miss Palmer's, as a boarding student, is that you will sometimes feel extraordinarily *lonely*, sad, or homesick. If you get weak and tell your roommate, who you will naturally regard as "family," and share your feelings in the *strictest confidence*, it is very likely that by noon at least half the school will know your deepest, dirtiest little family secrets.

I had more confidence in Clarissa. She was different than the other girls here. Everyone knew the British were a nation of ethical, stiff-upper-lip folks. I would have to seriously consider telling her about what happened with my father on another evening over candy corns and more tea and whiskey.

I excused myself to go down the hall to the restroom. I could hear someone in the far stall throwing up.

At least I wasn't alone. I can't tell you how many girls I heard puking their guts out around here, usually because someone started a smear campaign against them. Recently, the targeted taunting of secret-society bitches caused freshman Nicole Brightman to become so anorexic she had to leave the school and be hospitalized. Every week, we had girls stop eating normal meals in the dining room and start living on crazy self-styled diets like only eating celery and tahini, or Diet Cokes and beef jerky. A girl on my floor, Amy Atkins, ate charcoal sticks and swore they aided in digestion and would help keep her thinner. The cacophony of choral vomiting after lights-out was sickening.

This was all either directly, or indirectly, caused by the unrelenting pressure of the school, the emotional isolation, and the girls' inner desires to be loved and fit in. In my case, I couldn't tell you if it was due to my parents being fitness freaks my entire life, Mom accusing Dad of touching me inappropriately and sending me to Miss Palmer's School, or the constant scrutiny of the secret-society bitches, or as they officially referred to themselves — the Oprichniki.

The Spark

• • • • • • • • • •

THE MOST PERILOUS social reality at Miss Palmer's School was the deeply disturbing secret society referred to as "the Oprichniki." Some of the girls said it meant "Oprah-rich-Nikki" referring to a member whose father was as rich as the television star, Oprah. Actually, the girls were inspired by a sixteenth-century group of secret police employed by Russian Tsar Ivan the Terrible, the *Oprichnik,* to destroy his enemies. It is believed his second wife, Maria Temryukovna, actually came up with the idea.

Make no mistake: the school did not officially recognize the Oprichniki as a social club.

The day you arrived to Miss Palmer's School, the Oprichniki measured you. Were you attractive, bright, dumb, fat, thin, stylish, rich or poor? The rich, pretty, smart, and thin girls comported themselves with the most confidence. The short, chubby, socially awkward, or outwardly different became immediate targets. The Oprichniki believed its unofficial social responsibility was to serve as the school's arbiters of decorum and style. If a girl were too fat, or too thin, she would have to be fixed. The bottom line: *those unwilling to improve must be removed.*

Their goal was to make the "odd-girls-out" feel so bad they would want to leave the school. Many Palmer girls came from divorced parents, with one or both parents being alcoholics. And most had some kind of crazy family secret involving drugs, sex, or financial scandal. It was pretty clear that one didn't talk about it and one should act as if everything in one's life, and one's family's lives, was fabulous. If a girl got weak and shared too much personal information, one or all of the Oprichniki would find a way, as we said back home, to *put you on blast*.

When I arrived my freshman year I was super tan, wore short multi-color cotton skirts, tiny tops, cool handmade shell jewelry, and flip flops. This was quite a fashion imbalance on the usual Miss Palmer's School scale of uniformity: slender pale girls in plain, baggy clothing, t-shirts or sweatshirts with Ivy League college names, and little make-up or jewelry. And the most difficult to stomach: tennis shoes, UGGs, or some other stupidly sensible footwear.

At first, the other girls didn't bother me, as they assumed I must be the child of a famous Hollywood actor and let it slide, with a watchful eye to see if I would fall into place. I changed my appearance and got really involved in sports, where I tended to be stronger and faster than the other girls, and they left me alone.

I struggled to appreciate the New England landscape, a sharp contrast to my Pacific beach life back home. Instead of white sand, boardwalks hugging the ocean, and contemporary architecture dotted with palm trees and canals, Connecticut was all narrow roads, fluffy trees, quaint flower gardens, paved brick walkways, historic rectangular red-brick homes with Colonial shingles and black shutters, and oh my God—snow!

The most disturbing contrast was not environmental, or even visible to the naked eye. It was the simple, yet profoundly disturbing, philosophical concept that characterized Miss Palmer's social reality—*duality*. That is to say, as much as the school insisted that we maintained a strict honor code that upheld honesty, and respect for others and their property and opinions, these well-heeled Oprichniki girls were some of the most clandestine, duplicitous, thieving little bitches I had ever known.

While my roommate Clarissa was categorized by the Oprichniki as "different," she was enchantingly beautiful, of royal blood, and more experienced in the ways of living abroad. That insured the older girls didn't dare tangle with Clarissa. Her differences in manner or dress were found exotic, rather than undesirable and in need of "adjustment." Clarissa had the infectious habit of saying, "quite," both as a punctuation point and as a facetious stab to the neck. I often heard the other girls excitedly telling her amusing quips and follies to gain her approval, asking, "Isn't that amazing?" More often than not, Clarissa would give a superior smile and air of amusement and simply say, "Quite." Which was her way of inferring that the speaker was ridiculous and utterly boring.

• • •

Clarissa had been too busy with late evening play rehearsals to inquire further about my family life. With our total enrollment just over three hundred girls and an average class size of twelve students, you can imagine the gossip that went on between classes. I got out of Comparative Literature class — or 'Clit," as we referred to it — and walked across campus to have lunch at the Student Center. I saw Clarissa gathered with a group of high-level Oprichniki girls outside the front. I recognized Katherine "Kate" Cunningham, one of the most vindictive, sadistic bitches in the entire *not-so-secret* secret society. She was flanked by two of her "Yes Miss Kate girls," Kitty and Bunny, and a new girl I didn't recognize beside Clarissa.

In passing, I heard Bunny say, "Can you believe that Ralphie. What a train wreck!"

Kate added, "Well, it serves that little porno princess right for hanging out with townie scum boys!"

"What did she do, for Christ's sake? Tell me!" Kitty demanded as she slightly stamped an UGG.

"Well, last night, Ralphie was invited out with a townie boy named Kirk. Apparently, he heard about her infamous instructions to help Miss Palmer girls on how to give the perfect blowjob. He couldn't wait to see if the instructor was as enthusiastic as her pupils." Bunny concluded with a moment of self-amusement and a strange muffled chuckle that never left her windpipe.

"Then, Kirk took Ralphie to none other than our local Farmington King of Hip Hop's house for his new CD release party. It seems his lordship, P-Real, was enamored with Ralphie and invited her to take her clothes off and swim in his enormous pool, purportedly in the actual shape of his penis! Well, Ralphie is a *total talker* and had no intention participating in *that fun*, and certainly had no intention of sharing her professed licky-kissy-swallow skills with *anybody* at that pool party.

"To avoid potentially dangerous social interactions with strangers, Ralphie went to the kitchen and found some delicious brownies and committed herself to eating a great many. What she didn't know was just how much marijuana was baked into them and in no time, she was flying. According to the porno pool party film that Kirk posted online, Ralphie did join in after all!

"She got back to school too late for last call and decided to climb two stories up a tree and bang on Judy Bennett's window. When Judy opened the window, Ralphie lost her balance on the snowy ledge and fell."

"Oh my God, did she die?" Kitty blurted out uncontrollably.

"No, through the grace of God, she broke her fall in a big snow mound, resulting in a fractured ankle, broken arm, and school suspension."

"Well, serves the little fool right for fraternizing with Farmington negroes and townies." Kate said tartly.

After this comment, I was out of earshot and went into the building disgusted by what I just heard. *How could Clarissa be keeping company with a tribe of backstabbing, heartless, and racist bitches? Were they recruiting her for the Oprichniki?* Just before I went inside the building, my eyes locked with Clarissa's and I don't know if she was being capricious, or trying to tell me something, but she gave me a long, silent stare with a strange, tacit Mona Lisa-like smile. As the door closed, I saw Clarissa talking with a great deal of conviction and passion, which made me feel sick.

"You racist cow, how can you stand yourself?" Clarissa said, looking Kate directly in the eyes. "Are you mad as a bag of ferrets? 'Farmington Negroes and townies'… are we in the antebellum South? Is this fucking Tara? You stupid little West Texas twonk!"

And that is all it took to turn the entire Oprichniki sisterhood against Clarissa. She truly had no idea what was coming. Within twenty-four hours, Kate had her agents in every corner of Miss Palmer's rummaging for information that could be used against her and cause collateral damage—me!

As it turns out, Kitty had been in gym class with Clarissa when Coach Bergen made all the girls lift weights. Clarissa nonchalantly mentioned to Kitty that it should be "Bar Darling" teaching us all this—she is a pro!" Of course, Clarissa thought nothing of it. However, Kitty thought rather a lot about it. Kate had given her marching orders to find "any means necessary to destroy Clarissa." Kitty did some poking around and discovered a number of photos on the Giggle search engine of me with my famous bodybuilder parents in Venice, and just by chance, the early digital cover promo for the upcoming *Muscle & Fitness* magazine. A diamond mine discovery for any truly talented extortionist or, seasoned Oprichniki scout.

Kate saw this as an excellent opportunity to stick it to Clarissa *indirectly*, knowing full well it could cause a cataclysmic schism in our new dorm-room sisterhood. In moments like these, anything could happen: accusations, screaming and tear shedding, and even the occasional trip home.

When I returned to our dorm room that evening I had a little surprise waiting for me. On my side of the room, next to my bed, was a resplendent new decorative wallpaper treatment:

wall-to-wall blown-up images of bodybuilder cutouts from various magazines featuring my mom and dad. An enormous extra-glittery banner read, HERE SLEEPS BARBELLA, DAUGHTER OF BARBIE AND DUMBBELL.

My first reaction was to find Kate Cunningham and kick her ass. My second was to rip Clarissa's beautiful, wavy blonde-haired head off her body and put it on a stick and parade her around campus like some kind of medieval adulterous wench. And thirdly, to reach under my bed and shovel mounds of candy corns into my mouth. With every handful, I was growing more upset and desperate to know the truth.

Obviously, Clarissa had to have told Kate about my parents. How else would she know? How was I going to be able to face Clarissa? How was I going to be able to live with her the rest of the year knowing that she is both a liar and a traitor!

Clarissa would be home late from rehearsal. I didn't want to talk to her tonight. I couldn't. I left the photos of Mom and Dad up on the wall to remind myself to trust no one, to remember where I came from, and to show those Oprichniki bitches that they couldn't knock me down.

But inside, I was devastated.

In spite of my anxiety, I had a new feeling germinating inside that was as foreign to me as waking up in Paris: a strange sense of pride about who I was and were I came from. I lay staring at the photo collage of my mom and dad, and something about seeing all those images together spread out in front of me, and remembering all those years back in Venice—Gold's Gym, the beach, Mama DeySarkar, Uncle J.J., and the smell of chicken, broccoli, and sweat—woke up something in me as fundamental as a bench press set.

I could hear Dad say, "Come on, kid, you can do it—you got this—you are tough!"

Reconciliation

• • • • • • • • • • • • • •

OVERNIGHT, MY PET name at school went from Bar, to Barbell. And actually, that was the perfect name, because I was becoming tough as steel. Any and all interest in fitting in with these little tidy backstabbing bitches left me. I was officially angry. I made it a point to befriend the most socially awkward, displaced girls, as well as every girl that checked "other" on *Country of Origin* on their application to Miss Palmer's School.

Clarissa had been too busy with her play to even notice I was giving her the serious freeze. I almost let her have it when she said, "Oh, I love what you've done with the place." That was Clarissa speak for *Bar Darling, it is interesting that both your parents are muscle motivated, but really darling, do you feel this is their best location for display?*

Every place I turned, one of the Oprichniki girls purposefully placed themselves in my path. Tuesday and Thursdays, I sat next to Kitty in my American History class. Kitty spent the hour staring at me in a vile, psycho-brat manner that suggested, *It was me that nailed you bitch and there is more to come.*

I think our teacher, Mrs. Claiborne, is a clairvoyant, because she asked me to sit beside her and announced to the class I would be her new teaching assistant. This pleased me — in my new role I would assist in grading papers, which was a terrific opportunity to destroy Kitty one ill-conceived idea, run-on sentence, and misused comma at a time. While Kitty was a nearly perfect-looking petite brunette, her academic performance reflected that of someone who had suffered several serious falls off a pony as a child. Further, she suffered from panic attacks when forced to speak publicly.

Every other day, I ran into Kate Cunningham, who I now referred to in my mind as Kate Cunt-ingham. Her favorite thing to do was wait until there was a large group of Oprichniki and hangers-on and whistle to get my attention, and then mime curling a barbell. The other little bitches would chime in with, "Go, Kate, you can do it—curl it baby!"

I was adamant not to retaliate and determined that I would finish the year in peace and all this would blow over by senior year. I would graduate and move on to college and away from all of this sophomoric crap.

• • •

A couple of weeks later, with no real blasts from the Oprichniki, I felt like everything had gotten back to normal. Clarissa was usually rehearsing late for her upcoming performance in *Pride and Prejudice* as the future Mrs. Darcy. One night she came in really late—and I think slightly drunk—and jumped in bed with me, scaring the hell out of me.

"Bar Darling," she began, "I know I have caused you an enormous upset and I am truly, no—*dreadfully*—sorry. I don't fully understand what I've caused, and frankly I don't even know who, or what, these Oprichniki *bugger-all* prats are, or why they have selected you to humiliate. Can we not discuss this and work it out, darling? I miss our little tea parties and pillow chats."

I threw my blanket over my head. "I am asleep!" But she wouldn't let up.

"Bar Darling, we Westwicks haven't been made to formally apologize since the times of Edward the Third, and even then, it was some marginal offense related to hunting the King's favorite guinea fowl 'round Christmas, or some such rubbish. Tell me, what *must* I do, darling? I am bent on sorrowful knee, begging you to forgive me for whatever foolish *faux pas* I have committed."

It was obvious she was being sincere and relentless. So I flipped off the comforter. "OK, but we have some things to get straight first!"

Clarissa squeezed me. "Oh thank God, let's have some tea and a chat! This bloody snowstorm will surely cause first class to be canceled tomorrow."

"OK, but we are going to have to be *very* quiet. I would hate for you to be cast into Pete's dungeon tonight."

"Well, *that* won't happen, regardless of how much feminist literature I devour. So, Bar Darling, what do we need to *straighten out?*"

"Have you been invited to join the Oprichniki?"

"The what? I don't even know what that is…"

"Well, it is the 'secret society' that Kate and her friends are in. After I told you—in confidence—about my parents being bodybuilders, I saw you talking to them excitedly in front of the Student Center, and shortly after that my room was postered by the Oprichniki, and Cowgirl Kate is targeting me for public ridicule."

"So, you think that I conspired against you? Do you actually think I would join a club of duplicitous dilettantes? Oh darling, you don't know me very well, and for that I am sorry. I have failed you both as a friend and roommate.

"I frankly can't stand the idea of a secret club and certainly wouldn't join theirs. I made a dreadful mistake. I *accidentally* made a comment while in gym class. Coach Bergen insisted we lift weights to improve our volleyball slams. We were all miserably lacking in technique, and I simply said under my breath we should have you teach us because you were a pro. I had no idea someone would actually hear me, much less research my comment and use it against you. Bar Darling, I am truly sorry to have caused such a row with those silly girls."

"Wow, I am so relieved to hear you are not joining them. I think I've been the bad friend."

"Right, darling, let's put this all behind us, shall we? As I recall, before all this turbulence, you were telling me why you selected Miss Palmer's School."

As good as it felt to get that straightened out with Clarissa, I still felt a little raw emotionally. I could have easily fallen back asleep, but Clarissa had already made tea and seemed so genuinely concerned about our friendship. So, I decided to trust her.

"OK, Miss Clarissa, the story of Barbella."

"Oh goodie!"

"My Grandmother Pippa, my mother's grandmother, died and left me an educational trust fund. It stipulated that I had to attend Miss Palmer's School and then go on to Yale. Without her gift, my parents couldn't even afford to send me to community college. But the real reason Mom encouraged me is absolutely between you and me. Can you do that for me, as my friend?"

"Yes, of course, darling!"

Without realizing it, I grabbed one of my pillows and put it in front of me over my stomach and squeezed it. Clarissa could sense my anxiety and smiled reassuringly.

"OK, well, as you already know, my mom and dad are both bodybuilders. Actually, technically Mom is a body-sculpting model and Dad is the bodybuilder."

"Darling, sorry to interrupt, but what is the difference?"

"Steroids! Mom doesn't take them and Dad does, because he competes. In today's world, if you want to compete and win, you have to take steroids. It is really messed up… The other important part of the story is… well, I'm an accident."

"A lovely one, I might add!" Clarissa punctuated sweetly. "So what is that about?"

"My parents met in a sandwich shop in Venice."

"Italy, how romantic?"

"No, Venice Beach, California. Mom was from Manhattan."

"Oh, a big-city girl!"

"No, Manhattan, Kansas. She got a job as a flight attendant and was based in Los Angeles. One day she bumped into my Dad at the Sub Shop and he told her he had 'noticed her working out' at Gold's. That's all it took, and Mom was knocked up as fast as it takes Arnold Schwarzenegger to curl a barbell!"

"So when did they get married?"

"They didn't. They lived together for a short time and mom was always making him lunch and bringing it to him at the gym. While she was still pregnant with yours truly, she brought him lunch at Gold's and caught him in the alley with a new female bodybuilder from South Africa named Delicia. I guess he found her too *delicious* to pass up."

"I'd say, my God. Did you go to Gold's Gym as a little girl?"

"Did I go? I was raised in the gym! I went with my mom. I went every Tuesday with my dad. Of course, we all did. That's how I got my name. Dad use to joke with Arnie at the gym and yell out, 'The Austrian Oak may curl a barbell, but The Italian Rock curls a *barbella!*' Of course, in his mind, like all things it linked back to the beauty of hot blondes, Barbies and muscles, barbells, not to mention the sexy leading lady in the film *Barbarella*, as played by Miss Fonda."

Clarissa cleared her throat, more to buy a moment of time to absorb what she had just heard, and slowly leaned toward me. "If your mother was working for the airlines when you were a baby, did your father take care of you all day?"

"No, he was *always* training. I don't think you understand. Our lives revolved around my Dad's workout schedule: Up at three-thirty a.m., eat oatmeal and toast, start training by four a.m. An hour and a half later, six egg whites and a boiled chicken breast. Resume workout, eat three hours later, work out, and eat three hours later.

"For the first two years of my life, Mom dropped me off at a neighborhood babysitter named Mama DeySarkar's house. I couldn't pronounce her name, and so I referred to her as 'Mama Day Sucka.' She plopped me down next to her own chubby kids in a giant crib in front of a huge color television. Every day at eleven a.m., Mama DeySarkar would watch the afternoon classic Bollywood film extravaganza. We all tried to dance like the cast of colorful dancers. Then to put us to sleep for our naps, she played a beautiful evening raga by an amazing Indian flautist named Hariprasad."

"Oh that is brilliant! Did she prepare Indian dishes for meal times?"

"She would feed us these exotic curry dishes that left stains on all of my play clothes."

"So then what happened?" Clarissa nudged.

"Mom had several male roommates. First, there was 'Uncle J.J.' He was very tall and thin with a long nose, and big puffy black hair. He from New York City and moved to California to become a professional comedian. He was Jewish, but talked like he was an Italian mobster in an old black-and-white movie. He would say things to me like, 'Hey you—yeah you kid—get ova here!' I only remember laughing for the first four years of my life."

"Darling, I only remember crying for the first four years of my life because our nanny was straight out of a horror film! What happened after Uncle J.J. left?"

I started to feel really vulnerable the more I talked. I realized I couldn't just stop talking, and eventually I would get to the really difficult part. I found myself speaking faster and giving silly random details, saying anything that came to mind to keep her away. "There were other roommates, mostly bodybuilders, but a few years later, 'Uncle Matty' moved in. I loved him. He was a special-needs teacher, but to see him walking on the beach, you would think he was a movie star. He liked to walk down the Boardwalk in his bright yellow Speedo bathing suit and as he liked to say, 'get my walking-around tan!'"

"Darling, that all seems rather fun and pleasant."

I burst into tears and buried my head deeply into my pillow. After a few moments of sobbing, I continued my story. "It was fun, until one of my Dad's idiot ex-girlfriends told Mom that she thought Dad touched me 'inappropriately.' And then, all hell broke loose."

Clarissa reached over gently and touched my wrist and grabbed my hand and held it tightly. She didn't have to say anything for me to know that she was assuring me that she was my friend and would not betray my trust.

"I don't remember him doing anything creepy, but I do remember him being really physical and sexual with women. Being Italian, he kissed, hugged, and touched a lot. My entire life he liked to pat me on my bottom and petted my head. Whatever really happened, Mom treated Dad like he was a rapist and he went crazy, and that ended our Tuesday trips to Gold's. In fact, that ended all contact. He was so humiliated by her accusation he completely cut contact with me all together. Plus, he had me banned from the gym. It was like God kicking you out of church! I was devastated."

"You darling girl. That is dreadful. So you still haven't spoken to your father?"

"No, not a word in over two years."

"Poor dear, you must be exhausted from talking about all this."

"Yeah, I'm really tired, but I have to ask you something, Clarissa. Truly an enormous favor."

"Anything, darling, well, short of a sleepover with Pete!"

"Promise me that you won't talk about this with *anyone*."

"I do so sincerely promise, Bar Darling."

"And, will you help me get those Oprichniki bitches back?"

"Of course, darling, with tremendous pleasure. Or, as you like to say in America, let's *kick some Oprichniki ass!*"

Senior Year

• • • • • • • • • • •

CLARISSA WAS PARTICULARLY motivated to help me wage war on the Oprichniki after learning that she too was on their hit list. Kate started a rumor following Christmas break that Clarissa had slept with a young German aristocratic billionaire, Prince Albert Von Thurn und Taxis, back in England.

When I asked her if it was true, she simply cocked her head, smiled churlishly, and said, 'Quite!' Which was Clarissa's way of saying, *Well, it could be true, but even if it were, it is clearly none of your business and I have no intention of telling you straight out, but as you are my roommate, frankly, yes I did, but we will not discuss the sticky bits — end of discussion.*

Our first order of business was to get our new war room ready. We moved to the Caldwell Home dorm for seniors. The next priority was to target the newly appointed queen bee of the Oprichniki, the diva of the Hintly House dorm: Miss Kate Cunningham from Tyler, Texas.

Kate's dad was dripping in New Oil, but she marched around like she was a Standard Oil heiress, a Rockefeller. Our first retaliatory strike involved researching a bit more about Kate's background. Clarissa suggested an online genealogy search, and within one hour we had enough information on her lackluster nouveau riche family to seriously embarrass her. It seemed that her grandma, Bertha Cunningham, was famous for running the only bar and brothel in the miserable dry county. She raised enough money for her son to start wildcatting for oil.

Of course, we too had a little art party to redecorate Kate's room. This involved painting a magnificent mural with longhorn cattle, oil wells, cactus, a saloon, and dancehall hookers with a banner in the center that read HERE SLEEPS COWGIRL KATE. Clarissa composed a hilarious short story about Kate and her family, borrowing from any number of bodacious and concocted tales of the wild Texas frontier, including: how Kate lost her virginity to a miniature horse on the farm; shootouts with their neighbors, the Bush family; cattle drives to New Mexico; and even her great-great-grandmother's recipe, from Dime Box, Texas, for moonshine and rattlesnake pie. We left a copy of *The Adventures of Cowgirl Kate* under each girl's dorm door.

The next day, all the girls—less the Oprichniki—were calling her "Cowgirl Kate" and making mooing sounds when she walked across campus. I realize that doesn't seem very harsh, but when every breath is dedicated to being socially prodigious, it is *huge*.

Our victorious attack was celebrated for only a short time, as Kate made it clear she would hit back hard. Not only did she use every waking moment dreaming up ridiculous lies and making pestilent, passive-aggressive comments, she had the entire Oprichniki-sneakies on high alert. Everywhere I turned, some little secret-agent bitch was watching me, studying my every move. Life on campus became very unpleasant. My stress level was so high I could hardly keep anything in my stomach. Of course, purging candy corn nightly wasn't helping matters at hand.

• • •

In the early part of the spring an unexpected pleasurable occurrence came into my life: Dean began to feverishly flirt with me.

He worked at the packy, a combo package store and gas station where we all went to buy junk food and cash checks. Dean was a celebrity at Miss Palmer's. He was the only sexy guy under twenty within a forty-mile radius. He was as tirelessly horny as he was beautiful. He had long wavy, brown hair and big blue eyes that seemed to convey that any woman he talked to was beautiful and important to him. He was trim and solidly built, with tan arms, long thick fingers, pronounced triceps, and a couple unusual tattoos. On him they looked enigmatic, especially the small line drawing of a sailboat on his left inner forearm.

All the girls were happy to excuse the grease under his fingernails in the service of an exhilarating quickie in the stockroom. Apparently, Dean had a gift for being able to get erect instantly, enjoy several minutes of jaunty passion play and explode, all before the next customer was able to reach the window to pay. It seemed to give new meaning to the term "pump and pay."

One day, when I went to the packy for my weekly mountain of candy corns—which I told Dean would be shared among the girls on my floor—he began to work on me.

"Oh hey, you are Barbella, right?"

"Yeah, how did you know?"

"I've seen you in here with that English girl."

"Yeah, she's a real beauty," I said, certain he was trying to get information about Clarissa to strengthen his interest in seducing her.

"Not as *real* as you," he said with a deliciously neutral smile.

I panicked. *What did that mean? That she is the beauty and I am "real," as in a real girl-next-door and a trustworthy pal?*

"Well, thanks. Take it easy." I said, trying to leave quickly.

"For sure, oh hey, would you like to hang out here with me for a bit? We could eat candy corns and…"

"Wow, that sounds great, but I have an English class in twenty minutes and have to run."

"Well, maybe another time? We could read poetry to one another. Do you like to write?"

"Yes, I do. How did you know?"

"You just have that vibe, you seem really creative."

"Cool, see you around," I said in disbelief. *How did he know I like to write? Was he being for real? What did "hang out" mean?*

Given his reputation, "hang out" could mean only one thing. I nervously decided that if Dean was going to be *the one*, my first, because I accepted an invitation to "hang out," I had better be prepared for his amorous enthusiasm.

I tried to weigh the pros and cons. The obvious pro is that he was purported to be something of a "pro" himself, and that could make the first time less awkward. Some of the girls talked about their first time as if it was a nightmarish occasion: bleeding, crying, mistaken entrance identity, STDs, and the crown jewel of all unwanted post-frolic possibilities for a Miss Palmer's girl—pregnancy.

I wasn't a prude; I kissed plenty of boys back home, I just hadn't met a guy that I wanted to share *that* with. Somehow it never occurred to me that I would have sex at Miss Palmer's School. The very social fabric of the place felt like the antithesis of sensual invitation: no boys and plain-looking girls.

Clearly, sex was always a possibility, as we have known from the randy rogering of the teaching faculty, or any number of the townie boys. However, the usual townie date involved being taken to a "field party" and drinking copious amounts of Jungle Punch—basically a witches' brew comprised of mixing punch with Everclear, vodka, gin, and tequila. After a couple of glasses of this hallucinogenic, any Palmer girl would consent to being dragged deeper in the woods.

None of that had much appeal for me. I wasn't even sure what my sexual appetite was at the moment. Most of my sex fantasies, in the rare times that I allowed myself to have one, didn't even involve a person. Normally, I assumed that I was a Tasmanian platypus and swam freely through the warm salt waters in the sun. The sensuality of the water and the sun transported me to a special and personal place, far away from Miss Palmer's school and all her residents.

Over the next month Dean's attention blossomed: jovial exchanges, flirtations, and lingering smiles. Several of the girls knew about my attraction to Dean and supported the idea that I should *give it a go*.

On Easter Sunday, I went to the packy to pick up some more candy supplies. Dean didn't usually work on Sunday, something about having to help his mom with his sick grandmother with cancer. When I walked in, I was surprised to see him behind the counter wearing bunny ears.

"Nice ears!" I said.

"Well, as they say, you are no bunny, until some bunny loves you!"

"Cute. Why are you working on Easter Sunday?"

"My grandmother died." He sounded like a sad little boy.

"Wow, I am so sorry. You need a hug?"

"Sure, that would be great!" Dean walked around from behind the counter.

He looked so cute with his bunny ears and those big dopey, sad eyes. He held me tightly for a long time. His t-shirt smelled faintly of soap and his skin smelled musky and felt warm, and then something ignited. It was like a brush fire was racing through my thighs and burning my stomach muscles. I leaned against the counter and I could feel his penis getting hard and pushing against me. His tongue swirled around in my mouth slowly and I could hear my own breathing getting louder and louder as he grabbed my ass with his strong hands.

He didn't ask me, he just pulled me to the stockroom in the back and soon after I was lifted onto a Fuzzy Baby Ducks beer box. Before I could comment on the funny sounding name of the beer, he put his tongue back in my mouth and yanked my panties down around my ankles. Just as I felt his fingers touch me, I heard two loud resounding bells—*ding ding*!

At first, I was so disoriented I imagined the bells were in my head. Then I heard Dean say, "Shit, a customer!"

I pulled my jeans up as fast as I could, and then I heard a familiar voice announce herself in the store. "Hello, anyone working today?"

Oh my God, it's Mrs. Claiborne. I took a deep breath and walked out after Dean into the store. "Oh, hey Mrs. C... Happy Easter!"

"Why, Barbella, what a nice surprise. What are you doing today?"

I could tell by the way she asked me, she sensed something was strange and was thinking,

Why was a Miss Palmer's School student walking out of the stockroom of the convenience store, flushed and breathing heavily, with a boy on Easter?

"Well, it is ironic that we are meeting here today, because I am interviewing Dean for my extra-credit paper for your class."

"Really? What is the subject?"

"I am exploring the idea of socio-economic disparity in the American experience and the contemporary struggles of the working class."

"Wow, that is terrific, Barbella. I can't wait to read it, and thank you, young man, for sharing your experience with her!"

"Absolutely," Dean exclaimed, as if he were now an American hero.

"Well, I better run, I'm having Easter lunch with my husband's family today and we are running late. Just the twenty dollars for gas and aspirin, please."

"Yeah, I was just finishing up our interview and I have to get back to campus. Thank you Dean, very much, your insight is really interesting."

"Thank you, hope to see you again" Dean said crisply. I walked Mrs. Claiborne out of the store, not really clear about what just happened, and what it meant, but I did enjoy the adrenaline rush. I felt like a fuzzy baby duck!

Banging the Piano

• • • • • • • • • •

I COULDN'T WAIT for Clarissa to get back so I could tell her about what happened with Dean. I could think of nothing else. My new obsession revolved around two key questions: should I, *or shouldn't I,* have sex with Dean?

Clarissa had been invited to Miss Wescott's home for Easter Sunday dinner. Miss Wescott's invitation probably went something like, *"I would hate for you to be alone on such an important holiday, and it would be an honor if you would join me and my family."* Which really translated to, *"I would hate to lose the opportunity to find out if there is a possible endowment from your father."* And Clarissa would accept by saying, "Oh thank you, Miss Wescott, that is so generous." Which really translates as, *My God, must I spend the entire evening hearing your pathetic monologues about your educational standards and aspirations for the Miss Palmer girls and offering me your nasty little chemical-filled chocolate bunny candies for dessert without a claret to wash down their little heads?*

Clarissa got back before lights out, and I had time to tell her about my packy pleasures with Dean.

"So Bar Darling, basically you had a two-minute kiss, what are you going on about?"

"Don't you see, I have to decide if I am going to *do it.*"

"It Darling, is not *that* big of a deal—*just do it*—and with any luck at all, Dean will actually know a thing or two."

"Like what?"

"Oh God, you can't really be serious!"

"Yes, I am very serious—tell me!"

"Bar Darling, that is rather like asking me to explain what good democracy feels like. Actually, that is a good parallel. Good sex is like good democracy: everyone's voice is heard, individuals are empowered, and one's own rights are honored."

"What does that mean in sexual terms?"

"Bar Darling, I can explain it to you, but I can't understand it for you..."

And that was Clarissa's way of conveying: *I am exhausted and have no intention of providing a sexual education course this evening, or any other. Go get mauled like the rest of us and get on with it!*

Frustrated, I ate handfuls of candy corns and then excused myself down the hall. When locked safely in my restroom stall, I just sat a moment and thought about what I should do regarding Dean. The main door slammed into the tile wall and I could hear the voices of Kitty and Bunny echoing and laughing as they entered the restroom.

"Jesus, Kitty, you can't be serious," Bunny said, thrilled by some obvious bit of gossip.

"So help me God, I heard it from Mrs. Claiborne's own mouth tonight."

"Why did you go to Mrs. Claiborne's house for Easter?"

"I didn't. I went to my father's attorney's house, who insisted I join his family and his brother's family, which happened to include Mrs. Claiborne."

"Oh my God, tell me again, exactly what she said."

"OK, so they showed up late, beyond fashionably, and Mrs. Claiborne went on about how sorry she was, but she had to stop at the packy, or push the car, as it was on fumes. And she ran into one of my students and was concerned for her well-being. She had to stay and make sure the poor girl was not in some kind of danger."

"So, I asked who the student was and she said that it was Barbella and she was in the back of the packy with Dean, but it was all fine and she was—*get this*—interviewing him for a class paper."

"*Oh my God*, we have got to tell Kate!"

Both girls roared with laughter and it reverberated right into my very soul. When they left, I buried my finger as far down my throat as possible and thought, *I am going to nail you bitches*.

• • •

On Monday, I couldn't wait to finish class and get to the packy and see if Dean and I just had a moment, or if something more would flourish between us.

As I walked up, I could see Kate at the counter laughing and talking with Dean. It was obvious she was flirting; you could smell her pheromones from across the parking lot.

When I walked in, Kate made the fakest cheerleader squeal I've ever heard come from the mouth of a human being. It sounded more like a retarded dolphin. "Well, if it isn't Barbell!"

Dean looked at her innocently. "Actually, her name is Barbella."

"Oh Dean honey, I know that, but didn't Bar tell you about her parents?"

"Ahh, no."

"Well honey, Bar here comes from a distinguished pair of professional bodybuilders back in *California*."

"Wooh, that is cool," Dean managed to get out before Kate darted to the door.

"Well, Dean honey, I will see *you* soon!"

When that catty little two-stepper left the store, I mustered up all of my strength to compose myself and give Dean no indication of the fact that I wanted to personally pull every bleached-blonde follicle out of Kate's little Barbie-doll head. Fortunately, Dean was oblivious to what Kate was trying to orchestrate, but it was painfully obvious to me and I accepted the challenge: who would bang Dean first?

Dean looked at me with his enormous eyes. "So, Barbella, do you think you would like to hook up this Saturday night after I close the packy?"

I immediately envisioned being drunk and dragged into the woods. "What did you have in mind?"

"Well, I think my mom is going out. Maybe you could come over and watch a movie or something."

"Well, that sounds great, but I have to be on campus by curfew and you will still be working, so if you are brave enough, you could sneak on campus and we could meet in the music hall and hang out. Do you know where that is on campus?"

"Yeah, sure, that is where my mom drags me every year to hear the Miss Palmer's choir sing Christmas carols."

"Great! How about at eleven p.m. Is that cool?"

"Totally."

I could feel my feel my blush begin in my toes and travel rapidly to my cheeks. I gave Dean a huge smile and left the packy and ran all the way back to my dorm. There was planning to do. I didn't want my first time to be on a foldout audience chair, on top of the piano, or on the cold terrazzo floor. I would have to solicit lookouts and make minor preparations for some kind of bedding to put under the piano. Clarissa agreed to help me and to recruit some trustworthy chums to keep watch for campus security guards on Saturday night. It was all so exciting.

On Saturday night, every detail was worked out to perfection, and our "watch party" guarded strategic posts around the building while Dean made his way covertly onto campus. Everything was going without a hitch. Dean, being the romantic, brought a bottle of whiskey he stole from the packy and some random wildflower that he must have snapped off a bush on the way over, as the end of the stem was mangled. He gave me a big hug and a warm kiss and seemed truly happy to see me.

I pointed to the piano. "Sir, I have prepared a private lounging area for your comfort." Dean smiled and followed me happily under the piano.

I would love to report that Dean's virtuosity in playing felt as romantic as Debussy's *Clair de Lune* under that piano. But sadly, it more closely resembled a spastic boy playing rugby, or a child banging the ivories.

At first, Dean was trying to be romantic. He was gently touching my shoulders, kissing me lightly on my cheeks. He stroked my hair and smiled into my eyes.

"You are so beautiful. I love your eyes."

I'm sure I blushed, but it was so dark, I didn't understand how he could see my eyes.

The more he rubbed against my leg, the more excited he got and within no more than a couple of minutes the romantic portion of the proceedings was clearly over. He asked me if I was on the pill, and I said no. Then he fumbled around to find his wallet and pulled out a condom and hit his head on the strings of the piano, sending an eerie *zang* sound that reverberated throughout the music hall.

When Dean placed his body over me, I began to hear strange sounds coming from the dark auditorium. At first, I thought is was Dean's moans, and then I realized it was ape sounds that started very softly, occasional *Uhh* and *Ugh* sounds, and then the entire hall began to sound like a party of chimpanzees screaming in the jungle, followed by uproarious laughter. Just before all the girls ran out of the hall, I heard an undeniably familiar voice among the group. It was the only girl in school that used the word, "Y'all."

I heard that twangy little Texas Oprichniki bitch say, "Y'all hurry!"

With all of his tongue thrusts and enthusiastic penetrations, I hadn't noticed the video camera that had been placed under the piano. I suppose the only real saving grace was that it was too dark in the recital hall to record any personal details. Surely Dean's long hair and his ravenous tongue down the back of my throat protected my identity. Or so I thought.

On Monday, as I was walking to class, I heard an anonymous girl in a crowd behind me scream, affecting a lower-class Bostonian accent. "Hey, Bar, what'da you say, let's all go to the packy and play the piano!" The Oprichniki had ensured the video had reached every girl in school. It was entitled DUMBELL LEARNS TO PLAY ROCK-MAN-GET-OFF.

Ignoring Dean was really easy after our little recital, when Clarissa informed me she overheard Bunny telling Kitty that Kate had paid Dean a handsome sum of money to bang my piano.

Make no mistake—this was an act of war.

Prelude in C Minor

• • • • • • • • •

THE SHORT-TERM RETALIATORY action on my part, just to make myself feel *immediately* better, was a group effort that required generous donations and skilled negotiations. The first stop was to Gale Brecklin, who possessed the only known master key to every door on campus. Then, I collected used tampons from all the girls in our dorm currently experiencing the dreaded cramp monsters. After an arduous process of harvesting, sun drying, clear coating, and painting in bold primary colors, I crafted a stunning work of art. It was a mobile homage in the Alexander Calder style, and I hung it directly over Kate's bed.

To complement the design motif, the girls at the equestrian stables were kind enough to donate fresh, steamy cow plops and horse dung. This I carefully stuffed and sewed into the personalized white-linen-and-pink-thread monogrammed fashion pillows on Kate's bed, which was itself spray-painted blood red. I think it is safe to say that when Kate entered her dorm room, she could be heard cursing all the way back home in Tyler, Texas. I achieved instant artistic fame!

While this was truly a victory, it seemed to ignite an insatiable mean streak in both Clarissa and myself. Just as the Oprichniki wanted to make sure their victims realized they weren't just dealing with one girl, but a highly motivated team of equally minded bitches, we too intended for them to know we would win by any means necessary. Next on the list, we would hit Kitty and Bunny to let them know we meant business.

Mrs. Claiborne announced on Tuesday that we had a "surprise presentation." We were given two days to write a paper to be read in class on the following Thursday. The paper had to be written about something "unexpected" in the American experience.

As the teacher's assistant, I would have each girl's work turned in to me. I would decide which girls would present to the class first. Clarissa had the brilliant idea to write a paper for Kitty. The idea was that when Kitty turned hers in on Tuesday, I would exchange her paper for ours, giving Kitty quite a shock when she began to read. Clarissa took some vile Japanese porn story from the Internet and exchanged the identity to reflect Americans.

It was entitled *Unexpected Alien Sexual Abductions in America*, by Kitty Connelly. It began:

> One night in 1963, in a remote village outside of Santa Fe, New Mexico, a group of Catholic schoolgirls were en route to their annual choir competition. It was dark along the dusty two-lane highway, and the only light came from the plethora of stars dotting the sky. Suddenly, their bus began to shake violently and it was lifted slowly off the road, completely enveloped in blinding white light. The roof of the bus began to open, as if it were a sardine can being peeled off. Soon after, a sucking sound pulled one of the girls upward, slowly into a long shaft…

The story went on to describe the horrifying events that proceeded. Deep anal probing, which is the alien method of measuring one's intelligence and extracting their political assertions. It described new Martian technology that actually allowed the probe to adjust perfectly to the anatomy of the abductees' and featured a built-in self-dispensing, restorative, vitamin-enriched, aroma-therapeutic, no-mess lubricant, and other amazing sci-fi pornographic innovations.

BARBELLA

On Thursday, I was ecstatic with anticipation of Kitty's big presentation. I decided she would read first. When she came into class, she gave me her patented pouty baby-bitch look and threw her paper at me and snapped, "A-plus or die, Dumbbell!"

I just smiled serenely and quickly placed her paper on the bottom of the stack. When the last girl gave me her paper, I placed Kitty's new paper on top. Mrs. Claiborne strolled in and casually asked the class if everyone was ready to give the class some new and unexpected insight into the American experience.

"Well, Barbella, are we ready to begin the presentations?"

"Yes, Mame."

"Why don't you call the first girl to present?"

"Yes, Mame, I think we will go in the order of the papers. Let's see... the first is Kitty Connelly."

All the girls seemed to smile and chuckle at the same time. Not because they knew what was coming, but because, in general, no one liked Kitty and knew that she freaked out when she had to stand up before the class. Moreover, she was one of those girls that always looked as if life was a disappointment and no amount of designer clothing, exotic vacations or Argentine polo players would help.

Kitty grabbed the paper from my hand and mindlessly slapped it on the podium and stood in front of the class with an under inspired energy that conveyed, *Let's just get this over with.* Without pausing or collecting herself, she raced to begin announcing the title, "Unexpected Alien S..." And she screeched to a halt, stopping with remarkable dexterity right on the first syllable of the word "sexual," coughed and said, "Excuse me!" and re-announced the title as "Unexpected Aliens in America."

"That seems like a very relevant topic, Miss Connelly," Mrs. Claiborne assured Kitty, assuming that nerves had gotten the best of her.

Kitty was now turning red and switching her weight from one foot to the other.

"Would you like to continue?" Mrs. Claiborne nudged gently.

"Well, as you all know, like thousands of aliens cross our border every year. And they are taking important jobs away from real hardworking Americans…"

Kitty suddenly stopped. The most unexpected thing in the American experience *did in fact happen* at that precise moment. Kitty began to pee. It wasn't obvious to the class, but from my vantage point, next to Mrs. Claiborne, I saw an undeniable stream of urine begin to make its way down her white legs. Kitty burst into tears and ran out of the classroom with her alien sci-fi porn paper crumpled tightly in her fist.

Without skipping a beat, I just called on the next presenter.

• • •

Bunny was my next target. She would be a cakewalk to embarrass. She and I played on the lacrosse team together, and my locker was next to hers. Bunny loved to tell stories, and her network of influence extended all along the Eastern Seaboard from Palm Beach to Maine. She had an impeccable social résumé and equally impressive personal hygiene. Bunny was immaculate in every sense of the term.

Bunny's changing ritual was a well-polished routine. She began by opening her locker and laying out her fresh clothes. She removed her soiled garments and put them in a pink canvas laundry bag. She put her baby powder in front of her folded underwear. She wrapped herself in two thick monogrammed Egyptian white cotton towels and carried a third for her hair. She took a shower, carefully washing her hair, talking the entire time, and stopped on the way back to look in the mirror. "Oh, I look dreadful," she said, and returned to her story and her locker. Then she applied a gob of baby powder between her legs.

That afternoon, I waited until Bunny made her way to the shower. I exchanged her baby powder dispenser with wickedly strong itch powder. When she returned I watched her put enough powder on to give the impression of snowfall in the locker room.

I didn't stick around for the powder to take effect. But, from what Clarissa told me, Bunny had an *epic*-proportion *vagi-volcano* in her next-period science class, causing her to run out in tears. Ah, the sweet sound of victory.

Kate Cunningham was now beginning to realize that not only did she underestimate our retaliatory capabilities; the other girls were beginning see some tarnish on Little Miss Best in Show from Texas and her little sidekicks. Kate was growing more insane daily with her determination to destroy us. The entire student body could feel it and that tension caused the faculty to become suspicious. They didn't know specifically what was happening, but they knew *something* was about to blow.

Clarissa and I simply didn't care anymore, and that made us formidable opponents.

The Sting

• • • • • • • • • •

LATE SPRING WOULD be our best chance to finally obliterate Kate and the Oprichniki once and for all. That was when the girls prepared for the Wishing on the Ring Ceremony, in which each New Girl, a freshman, asks an Old Girl, a senior, to wish on her new school ring. It was usually an emotional avalanche of teary, meaningless pontificating and promises. It was truly a bizarre practice because the New Girl had no way of really knowing the Old Girl, so it was based entirely on social fantasy: "Oh, I simply adore the way Caroline comports herself… I want to be just like her when I am a senior."

The big question, what New Girl could we employ to ask Kate for her blessing, to blast her hard? We found the perfect candidate in Brook Berkshire. She was devastatingly beautiful, impossibly rich, and seductively gay. Brook's favorite thing in life—in fact her *raison d'être*—was to seduce straight girls into a walk on the wild side and let her, as she said, "sexy them up for sport!" Truly amazing was her skill at closing the dirty deed. She boasted a ninety-eight percent success rate.

Brook agreed to do it under one condition: if Clarissa would kiss her for thirty minutes alone in her room. Clarissa had been reading gobs of radical-feminist literature and was most recently enamored with a self-described "black feminist lesbian *mother poet*," Audre Lorde. Clarissa felt that she couldn't possibly understand her literary hero, or call herself a true feminist, if she didn't at least once taste the desiring lips of another woman, excluding the invitations of House Director Pete.

Learning from Kate's earlier failed efforts to film my *divertimento* under the Steinway with Dean, we realized that we needed to be someplace more visible, with more light, and a place that would ensure instant social ruin for Kate and the Oprichniki. That could be only one place at Miss Palmer's School—the Main: a historic redbrick two-story structure, with six white Doric columns, black shutters, four vertical brick chimneys, and the towering white widow's walk. It was the most iconic building on campus since the school's founding in 1843.

But how could we trap Kate in the most public building on campus? We were stumped until a minor miracle occurred. Clarissa read in the school paper, *The Serengeti*—which we called the "Sara"—that the campus *a cappella* group The Pirouettes were holding tryouts at the Main on the following Sunday, before the Wishing on the Ring Ceremony. That would be perfect because Kate was a member of The Pirouettes, while Clarissa was the newest member of the parody singing group The Pyro-ettes, whose sole purpose in life was to outshine and mock the other group. We needed some kind of diversion, something that would throw Kate completely off guard and set the stage for Brook.

Finally, it came to me while purging my third handful of candy corns. I was recalling my first week at Miss Palmer's and being taken to Miss Wescott's office. How inspired I felt, how I wanted to emulate her. Things had changed. I now had no interest in being like her, or any of the *carefully cultivated* at Miss Palmer's. And then, it hit me. Brook must seduce Cowgirl Kate in Miss Wescott's office! That was the place. It had to be in Miss W's office, as it was the only room on campus that was somehow sacred. It was the symbolic epicenter of the school. But how would we get Kate in her office with Brook?

I knew the Pirouettes always made the girls auditioning sing the aria *Nessun Dorma*, traditionally a male role, from the Puccini opera *Turandot*, just to throw them off. Clarissa had the brilliant idea to write a contemporary version that would allow young Brook, on the dance team, to choreograph a seductive companion dance. She was determined to curl Kate's toes, which everyone knew was possible as Kate had previous "sleepovers" with House Director "Pete" when she first arrived to Miss P's.

Besides, it was tradition for the New Girl to meet with the Old Girl before the ring ceremony to formalize their plan for the big moment. This would give Brook a chance to steal Kate away to Miss Wescott's office alone.

Well, almost alone.

Clarissa, Brook, and myself met every evening to rehearse the song, the dance and the filming of the seduction. It had to go like clockwork, or we would get kicked out of school. While none of us really cared, it was a matter of pride that we pull this off.

Brook borrowed a stunning traditional Indian dance costume from the drama department. She removed half of the length of material and added a slit exposing her midsection, which gave it a super sexy appearance. With Brook's long dark olive legs and flat muscular stomach exposed, and her enormous catlike burnt umber eyes and red plump lips glistening, Kate would be hypnotized as fast as a cobra with an Indian snake charmer.

We had to sneak off campus to rehearse to keep our plan from being found out. The only place we could find was in the stockroom of the packy. This seemed to thrill Dean, who always suggested that one, or all of us, should engage him in his forte for some fast-fun, no-obligation fornication. He was oblivious to how that video hurt me, and never felt the slightest need to apologize nor explain why he allowed Kate to use him. Poor Dean: such beauty, and such unfortunate scruples and brevity. *Quel dommage!*

The big day for our sting operation came as quickly as the new pollen in the air, and we couldn't have been more prepared. At one p.m. I made my way to the Main to enter Miss Wescott's office and set up my video reconnaissance. I covertly slunk down the hall and tried her office door, but my fingers squished together in an abrupt halt.

Oh my God, Gale Brecklin told me she could open any door and would have it open by noon. But it was locked. I ran around the building and tried the windows. Through the grace of God, the window in front of her desk opened with a quick push. I almost broke both of my arms falling inverted onto her office's wooden floor. I found the most strategic spot to film the seduction scene, behind her thick red velvet curtains. I practiced shooting test video with my phone until I remembered I had to unlock Miss Wescott's office door so Brook could bring in Kate after her seductive dance.

Just as I brushed by Miss Wescott's desk, knocking some papers off, I heard the door handle turn slightly and a key scratch at the lock.

My heart felt like it relocated to my throat. I snatched the papers up and tucked myself behind the curtain just in time to hear Miss Wescott on her cell phone laughing loudly and telling someone on the other line that she could find her itinerary quickly and let them know. The way she communicated let me know that she knew the person on the other line very well, probably a boyfriend.

"Yes darling, I think the plane arrives around noon on Tuesday, but I forgot which airline Joanne booked… let me just find that itinerary on my desk. Hum, funny, I can't seem to locate it."

I looked down in my hand, which held an itinerary from U.S. American Airlines. Miss Wescott didn't seem to notice the open window as she scanned all the piles of papers across her desk, continuously apologizing for the delay. After a minute, she declared that she would have to call Joanne and get back to him and swiftly left her office.

The Pirouettes set up in the middle of the Main's entrance. It was the most acoustically advantageous location for showcasing the stream of talent now lining up for their big audition. Clarissa and Brook went to wait in the ladies' room before joining the group, due to Brook's provocative costume, which she hid under a trenchcoat. The first girl brave enough to stand before the table of the stern-looking Pirouette choir members was Carolyn Armstrong, the tallest and horsiest-looking girl at Miss Palmer's.

When Kate gave her the green light to begin her audition, everyone became uncomfortably stiff as if bracing themselves, fully anticipating her performance to sound like a cacophony of whinnies and neighs. As Carolyn began to sing *Nessun Dorma*, her hypnotic, caressing tone, mesmerized the girls watching her performance. By the time she reached the uproarious conclusion of the third *Vincero*, every girl in the room was in tears.

As the ensemble group only had one spot in the choir open, all of the other girls waiting behind her in line applauded enthusiastically, turned in unison, and left the building. It was painfully clear no one could possibly beat Miss Armstrong's flawless performance. Kate stood up and firmly announced, "Well, ladies, I don't think we need to deliberate further, I think it is pretty obvious that we have our newest Pirouette! Carolyn, it is with great pleasure that we—"

Running down the hall, Clarissa uncharacteristically belted out, "Wait!" All of the Pirouettes snapped their attention and focus on Clarissa at the same time. "Ladies, if you please, I would very much appreciate the honor to audition for you. While Carolyn has sung beautifully, perhaps my interpretation might be of some interest. If you would be kind enough to allow me the chance to perform for you!"

Kate gave Clarissa an icy glare, and just before she could deny her request to audition, Beth Anne Dole, truly one of the nicest girls I had met in my life, piped up. "Why, Clarissa, we would be delighted to hear your audition." Because Beth Anne's father gave many millions of dollars to the school and owned one of the largest food companies in the world, Kate did not utter a word to the Princess of Pineapples.

Clarissa gathered her composure, took a deep breath, and assumed a dramatic position on her makeshift stage. Closing her eyes, she waited for a moment in silence for dramatic effect, and clapped her hands firmly twice. From the other side of the room, Nartana, the only Indian student at Miss Palmer's, entered in traditional costume, bringing with her the sound of tiny bells from her ankle bracelet, waking up the interest of all the spectators. She placed a speaker on the floor ceremonially. A dreamy Indian raga began to play and Clarissa again clapped firmly twice. Brook slowly entered, as if she were Salomé and would dance the seven veils for King Herod. She walked deliberately toward Kate and stopped, staring deeply into her eyes.

The music began to change with a slow rhythmic *tabla* drum, causing Brook to undulate with intoxicatingly sensual movement and expert charm. Then, Clarissa began to sing *Nessun Dorma* in a strange and surreal manner, almost monotone, yet pitch-perfect, without the usual dramatic rises and falls, allowing Brook's dance to be the focal point and passion of the performance.

Brook was so athletic in her dance movement that soon a slight sheen glistened on her lovely elongated neck and her thin muscular arms. The room felt hot and smelled of Brook's essence, perfuming the room with scents of vanilla, sandalwood, and lavender. Kate was utterly spellbound.

As the music and dance reached a feverish conclusion, Brook quickly whirled toward Kate, executing perfect *chaînés* turns, and stopped just before hitting the judge's table. She threw both of her hands perfectly into Kate's open palm, delivering a concealed note in a silk sash.

It took Kate a moment to come back to her senses as the crowd went mad with applause. Kate opened and read the note. After a long pause, Kate pushed herself up and said to Clarissa, "Well, Miss Clarissa, that was certainly some performance, now wasn't it, ladies?" The other judges enthusiastically agreed, and Miss Dole, unknowingly, audibly repeated several times, "Oh my God."

Kate continued, "While we must all agree that the today's performance was most impressive, vocally I am afraid we must remain with our decision to admit Miss Carolyn Armstrong. With that said, I would encourage Miss Brook to meet me after the auditions to discuss the possibility of becoming the Pirouettes' official choreographer this season."

Clarissa faked disappointment and left the building.

Brook swiftly guided Kate to Miss Westcott's office and by the time her fingers touched the knob, Cowgirl Kate was hers.

Brook silently removed several stacks of folders from Miss W's desk and directed Kate to sit on top with her back to the window. She removed her long, sheer silk veil and gently tied it around Kate's head, covering her eyes. Then she took the sash from around her waist and bound Kate's wrists together. She gently caressed Kate's thighs as she lightly kissed her neck. Kate began to breathe deeply and Brook could sense her fear and began to speak to her softly.

"Lovely, lovely girl…"

Kate, now lying flat on her back, and extending her bound hands over her head, whispered, "Yes, my little sultan." Brook moved her kisses slowly down from Kate's neck to her breasts and pulled up Kate's schoolgirl-plaid short skirt. She placed two fingers over Kate's panties. Kate began to move from side to side and Brook felt her relaxing into the rhythm of the fingers' movement.

I couldn't believe how clear it all looked on my phone video.

I decided to boldly sneak out from behind the velvet drapes and get a little closer to Kate so she could be clearly identified. Brook was so entranced that she didn't even notice that I was now in the center of the room. I almost broke out laughing because Kate's legs extended straight up—and spread—with Brook's head planted between them, the two looked like a big "W" on top of Miss Wescott's desk. It was all simply too perfect. On top of which, Kate was now saying crazy things like, "Oh yeah, baby... work, my little girly... Let me be your Oprichniki slave girl."

She was so clear and loud that it would be undeniably Kate's voice on the video and an admission of her involvement in the Oprichniki. I was feeling really excited. What I didn't expect was for the door to fly open and to hear Miss Wescott's voice sternly inquire, "Ladies, shouldn't you be preparing for the Wishing On The Ring ceremony?"

Out of utter horror, embarrassment, guilt, and some kind of bizarre subconscious auto-response, I said, "Oh, Miss Wescott, I found your itinerary!"

The Requiem

• • • • • • • • • • • •

MISS WESCOTT SENT a messenger with a memo on Sunday afternoon instructing Clarissa to be in her office Monday morning at 8 a.m., and for me to appear at 9, I knew I was going home. Clarissa wasn't in the room when the memo arrived; she was attending a presentation sponsored by one of the campus organizations, "Save Our Africa."

Instantly, that memo soured my surroundings. I was not going to miss all the subtle snobbery that was so deeply ingrained in most of the girls. They would be horrified if you identified any one of them openly as a "snob" or an "elitist." In fact, they would fiercely defend their position as citizens of the world.

They would explain that each girl is a dedicated member of a church youth group who was helping build wells for poor African villagers that didn't have fresh drinking water. Meanwhile, each girl's father invested in or ran a company that paid off officials for mineral and petroleum rights to extract as much wealth as possible *out of Africa.*

They might even have had a formidable humanistic crusade among the villagers, and displayed on social media all their photographs of the *real* Africa: traditional native costumes, mud huts, a few zebras, and the schoolhouse constructed from tree limbs and a dirt floor. They would excitedly return to school and discuss how profound the experience was and privately how cool they feel for having gone. Then, they would attend Yale, Princeton, or Harvard, or a smaller liberal arts school like Williams or Amherst, graduate, work, and most probably build their own family.

Africa would soon become a *fond memory*, lost in the shuffle of play dates, soccer practice, and other local charitable causes. Perhaps they would foster a love of African art, or make an annual $100 donation to a special group working with kids in Africa. But that girl will never truly invest in Africa. And in a very odd sense, these girls, and Miss Palmer's School, would become that for me, my *Out of Africa* experience, my little brush with the native elite: the eighty richest individuals on the planet who own the same as the poorest three-point-five billion.

• • •

On Monday morning, while I was waiting to see Miss Wescott, I couldn't help but feel melancholic. Leaving Miss Palmer's school in spring, before graduating, was not really what I had planned. Actually, I never had a plan, beyond attending Miss Palmer's School and Yale, but I didn't expect to get kicked out before graduating. Strangely, I began to feel sad about leaving. In a way, the school was the first time that I had ever had any discipline or structure in my life.

I would miss the New England seasons, the snow, and the equestrian stables. I would miss the deep dedication to education that was instilled by the wonderful teaching staff and the true fire for knowledge they inspired. They gave me a foundation, an unquenchable desire to learn, that I would be able to build upon regardless of where life took me. I was grateful to have had almost three and a half years of intense study, both socially and academically.

I had really grown to love Clarissa. I was going to miss all of her British poppycock and hearing her lovely voice. Well, that is, until I saw Bunny and Kitty in Miss Wescott's office. Bunny walked straight toward me, followed by Kitty. They sat beside me. Bunny cocked her head slightly and smirked.

"What do you want?" I asked.

"Well, Dumbbell, it seems that your little pranks have caught up with you!"

"You *think*?"

"No, I am fairly certain that you will be leaving campus this afternoon, and Kitty and I didn't want to miss the opportunity to say goodbye and to let you know something that we thought you might appreciate."

"Oh, by all means, *please do* share."

"Well, you see, the other day when you plopped into Miss Wescott's office and foolishly left her window open, Kitty and I just happened to be walking by and noticed the window opened, and soon after, we saw you in Miss Wescott's office." Bunny said, and then looked toward Kitty, who leaned across Bunny and continued talking.

"So, after we listened to Carolyn Armstrong's performance and were rendered to tears we went to the ladies room to freshen up. To our amazement, Clarissa was kissing some girl in exotic garb and we just excused ourselves and ran down the hall screaming. Well, as it happens Miss Wescott was entering the building and stopped us in our tracks for questioning and we felt it was our civic responsibility to let her know that we saw someone in her office."

Kitty smiled.

"Well, as you can imagine, Miss Wescott was full of questions and wanted to know more and we suggested that she should speak to Clarissa about what you might be up to, as you two are so close being roommates. As it happens, Clarissa was just leaving the building when Miss Wescott asked her to chat for a moment. At first, Clarissa said she had no idea where you might be, but when Miss Wescott suggested that she might find herself back in jolly old England, Clarissa suggested that she might try looking for you in her office."

"We are just devastated to lose Kate Cunningham as our leader, but we are so excited about our newly elected leader, Miss Bunny here, and of course, very excited about our newest nominated Oprichniki member—Miss Clarissa Westwick!"

Kitty and Bunny stood in unison and left the office.

I felt sick. I wanted to shovel candy corn in my mouth and kick down Miss Wescott's door and strangle Clarissa. *How could she do that to me? How could she do that to herself?* She obviously wanted to save her own ass. My mind replayed so many of our conversations and tea-party chats and then I remembered something she said recently, just before the big sting on Kate. I was commenting that I didn't even know why the Oprichniki existed.

"Bar Darling, in the end, none of this matters. Sadly, we are all made to play the game… a game that can change without notice."

When Miss Wescott's door opened, I was surprised to see that Clarissa was not there. She must have left before I arrived. Well, of course there wouldn't be much for them to talk about. She had already guaranteed her safety when she gave me up to Miss Wescott.

Miss Wescott was polite and formal about everything. She informed me that all of the arrangements had been made for my departure and that I would be leaving campus that day. The school arranged for someone to drive me to the airport, and my mother was already informed of my expulsion and would meet me at LAX.

The word "expulsion" sounded so nasty. It made me feel so unwanted. I went back to my dorm room and Clarissa was gone. On my bed was a note. At first, I ignored it. I knew that it was from Clarissa and I wasn't sure I could accept anything she told me. When I began opening drawers to pack, I imagined that I could hear her voice talking to me.

Everywhere I went in the room, it was as if she was there and talking. Finally, I went over and ripped open the envelope and read the note. It simply said:

Bar Darling, I am so dreadfully sorry about all this. You must trust that I didn't purposefully give you up. I will miss you terribly and hope that one day you will forgive me. With Love, Clarissa.

I put the note back in the envelope and tossed it into Clarissa's trash can. *I'll forgive you after I strangle you to death.*

Soon my anger and anxiety was taken over by a powerful sense of release and calm, with the feeling that I would be fine. As lost as I felt, I would be OK. It might be hard at first, but it would work out. I reasoned that I simply needed to find myself again, get the sand between my toes, smell the salty air and get back to something that felt real. No Oprichniki psycho-bitches trying to make me feel lesser than, no more stuffing candy down my throat and purging. I needed to leave the East Coast and Miss Palmer's School and go back to the land of the *bitchin bombies*. My home. Venice Beach.

Two

The Boardwalk

• • • • • • • • • • • • • • •

THE FIRST DAY HOME involved long, exhausting sessions of Mom screaming at me while I tried to explain why I was filming one girl feverishly licking another girl like an overzealous Jack Russell terrier on Miss Wescott's desk. Then came my crying sessions about why she had rented out my room—*my room*—to a neurotic female British bodybuilder named Tonya.

My only salvation lay in skateboarding directly to the Boardwalk.

The most unexpected emotions rushed over me when I arrived and the salty air whirled into my nostrils. I stopped and took a long, exploratory gaze. Venice seemed a bit seedier than I remembered it being. I guess after living in Farmington, Connecticut, anyplace would feel a little rough around the edges.

There was a circus of humanity walking on the sunny Boardwalk. A sidewalk symphony brought on by basketball players, disco roller skaters, vendors hawking their wares, boisterous nonsensical drunks, stoned homeless folks, exuberant street performers, skaters, and literally one hundred thousand tourists walking aimlessly. Not to mention the regular "characters" like "Hairy Terry," the rollerblading electric-guitar man; "King Mambo," the enormous gentle African wearing a tiny loincloth and multiple plastic snakes; or the adorable dwarf, dressed as a giant red heart, carrying a sign announcing FREE HUGS. It was all too overwhelming.

The Boardwalk was as natural to me as the blue sky, sun, sand, and palm trees. But now, I felt like a tourist. I didn't realize that, being held so firmly pressed to the bosom of Miss Palmer. Being told when to rise, eat, study, sleep, and socialize over the last several years had unknowingly caused me to view the world differently. I had caught an invisible social virus. I had become—dare I say it—judgmental. That was not who I truly was, but sadly it is what I allowed myself to become. After years of the Oprichniki scrutinizing my every action, as much as I thought I had resisted, I had forgotten how to be comfortable with humanity and most upsettingly, with myself.

Groups of young African-American males made me feel uneasy walking toward me on the street, as did the harmless homeless guys asking for some spare change so he could "buy some fuel for his jet plane," the hordes of chubby people eating pizza on the street, kids with crazy tattoos and piercings, and the loud families that poured into Venice in hope of seeing Arnold Schwarzenegger or a Hollywood "star." Even the ocean unnerved me slightly and I began to have irrational waves of thought. *What if we have a big earthquake? What if there is a tsunami? What if the drug lords from Mexico rush across the border and kill everyone and simply take all the cool homes for themselves?*

I felt vulnerable.

I decided to skate down to Muscle Beach to see if I could spot my dad, but I doubted it since he was now hosting a fitness television show on ESPN. He was probably at Gold's training, or with his girlfriend *du jour*. That was the funny thing about having a professional-bodybuilder father: you always knew where to find them—at the Gym. Sometimes, he and some of the other famous older bodybuilders went back to Muscle Beach just to excite the tourists and promote a new health product.

When I got there I didn't see Dad, just a strange assortment of old guys way past their prime, some ancient pro women bodybuilders that reminded me of Captain America in drag, and a couple of sunburned young guys from Germany who came thinking that the beach would be like it was back in the day, full of men with biggish biceps and bird legs filming themselves flexing.

I decided to head toward Gold's and see if I could get my frozen membership reinstated. There were so many tourists on the Boardwalk that I skated on the bike lane that curved and hugged the coastline. Shortly into my journey, skinny cyclists were screaming at me, "Get the fuck off the bike lane!" That was new. So, I jumped off at Sunset Avenue and made my way toward Pacific Avenue. It was great to see the bright fuchsia bougainvillea poking through the fences. They didn't have hot pink tropical flowers in Farmington, just pink polo shirts and matching hair bows.

At Main Street, I noticed a new fence that had cool wooden cutout designs over the chain link, and high-security cameras. I asked someone about to walk in the gate what it was and they just smirked and declared, "Giggle!" At first, I thought he was commanding me to giggle, but I realized he said it, as if to say *Really, you idiot, don't you know where God lives?* I almost fell off my skateboard. Giggle search engine moved to Venice? When did that happen? Giggle next door to Gold's gym, and they bought my favorite building in Venice: the Frank Gehry building shaped like binoculars. Holy Shit! Great, now we will have albino code junkies invading our public spaces talking about algorithms, Web security, and all that other programming crap.

Gold's

• • • • • • •

WHEN I GOT to Hampton Drive and saw the Gold's Gym logo, the two giant palm trees, and the muscle-posing-stand cutout at the front door, I started crying. All the time away, being estranged from Dad, arguing with Mom about my future, and all the memories of my childhood at Gold's, all of it converged inside my head. The realization that I was no longer a child was terrifying. It was time for me to take back my life and move on, but I had no clue what I should do. I was utterly lost. I had to stop and just let the tears flow.

When I finally felt calm enough to skate, I cruised into the parking lot, trying to avoid smashing into a $200,000 red Mercedes convertible waiting for a free parking space by the front door. When I walked in, I saw the pictures of Mom and Dad on the back wall, and noticed that the gym added rows of international flags hanging down from the ceiling. They had taken down a bunch of pictures of Uncle Arnold.

Then I heard a familiar voice yell out, "Ahh, Princess Barbella, where in the hell have you been? Welcome home!"

"Diego," I screamed and ran over to the counter and threw myself into his huge arms and squealed like a cheerleader. I instantly felt better.

"So, sweetheart, if you are looking for your pop, he is holding court with a busload of Japanese tourists out back, still dumbbell-benching two hundred—he's a freakin' animal!"

"Cool, I'll catch up with him later, but I just wanted to make sure that my membership is still OK so I can work off some of this Tootsie fat from school!"

Diego just smiled warmly. "Of course, angel. You will always have a lifetime membership here!"

I decided to run to the restroom before I headed out. I *did not* feel ready to see Dad. As I crossed the main room, that old familiar scent permeated the air: wet towels with a faint chemical aroma, male sweat, rubber, and steel. I heard the familiar grunts and sounds peppering the rap music overhead: intense breathing rushing spit and air into the front teeth, steel plates slapping, and trainers barking, "That's it, *come on*—give me two more—you can do it."

I felt all the muscles in my body yearn for that physical intensity. It was so innate; my entire life was formed around people's desire to build strength, muscle, and beauty. The moment I entered the women's locker room the desire for fitness stopped and the desire to eat candy corns began. What was happening to me? I felt like I was going insane. There was no one in the room. I went to the sink and splashed water on my face and looked at myself in the mirror. My eyes darted away from my image, and my inner voice began: *I need to get back in the gym. I will be OK. It will work out. God give me strength.*

The door of the ladies' room opened and I buried my face back in the sink. I must have been giving off some funky sad vibes because, I heard a woman say, "Hey, baby, are you OK?" I pulled my face up and saw the reflection of a beautiful African American woman wearing tiny, lemon-yellow workout gear posing in front of the mirror.

"Yeah, thanks. I'm just having a moment."

"I know what you mean. I've been working on my legs for two weeks and I still look like Skinny Minnie goes to the track meet."

"How often are you lifting?"

"I am at this stinky gym damn near everyday, and look at my guns..."

I dried my face and looked at her amazing body. She was flexing her arms in the mirror like an adolescent boy, trying to confirm a bicep muscle.

"What are you eating?" I asked.

"I have been lean and mean, just eating my veggies and sushi."

"Well, that may be part of your problem. Women don't produce the same level of testosterone that is necessary to develop the muscle mass you want, and you aren't eating nearly enough calories. You have to eat calories to produce muscle mass. Also, I can tell you are working your legs too much and avoiding your upper-body training."

"Well look at you, Little Miss Trainer. You are good at your job, and you are exactly right, 'cause I did not want to get me some big-ass man arms and shoulders."

"Don't worry, you won't unless you start doing steroids."

"Thank you so much. Now, I'm going to go eat me an enormous burger for lunch!"

"Sounds good. Enjoy."

When she left, it struck me like a lightning bolt. She just called me Little Miss Trainer. She said, "You are good at your job." *A trainer.* Of course, I am a trainer. I liked the sound of that. It made sense. I decided right then and there, that is what I would do with my life. As much as I loved the idea of attending a great liberal-arts university and becoming a writer, there was simply no money for that—for anything. Training was what I knew, and *helping others* was what I would do!

I felt instantly better and my brain went on overdrive about what I had to do to make this happen. One thing I like about myself is that when I made up my mind, and was clear about what I wanted to do, I moved my proverbial ass to get it done.

When I walked out of the locker room, the Japanese tourists had moved into the main room and had discovered the one and only Lou Ferrigno, "The Incredible Hulk," working out on the floor.

They had him surrounded, taking photos and saying, *"Sugoi... Kare wa honto ni okii desu ne."* Which translates to, "Wow—cool! He is really is big, right?" I laughed and headed for the door, waving goodbye to Diego.

Then I heard a deep familiar voice say, "Are you kidding me?"

And then I heard him sing the silly opera song he always sang when I was a little girl. "Bella, Bella, Bella, Barbella, where is my *piccola principessa*?" I felt a pain in my gut, turned quickly, starting to cry—and ran mindlessly into his huge chest and felt my feet leave the ground. He spun me around like a little rag doll.

I was dizzy for a moment, and he said, "Come on kid, I'll buy you lunch. I was going over to The Firehouse and we can catch up. Jesus, you look all grown up!" He had his arm around me and we were moving toward Rose Avenue, to eat at the restaurant where I had my first meal out as a child.

We sat outside and all the waiters that had worked at The Firehouse all these years came over and hugged me and said hi to my Dad, who was currently a "someone." Growing up in Southern California, *everyone* knows someone who is "someone," or is trying to be, or soon will be, or used to be. We all knew the illusion of it. Often, some nerdy little guy you went to high school with and never even noticed starts going to the gym, grows some facial hair, and the next thing you know he has a blockbuster TV series and he is suddenly a "sex symbol." Then he comes back to the neighborhood in an Italian racing car wearing a solid platinum watch with a diamond face.

In the bodybuilding world, being a *someone* meant winning contests, getting a sponsor, a role in a movie or television show—or, if you were an Olympian, a new product line. The product-line crap really pissed you off if you knew anything about health and nutrition.

The so-called health supplements are not regulated. They make $24 billion in annual income and essentially they are considered "healthy," unless the FDA proves that they are not safe, and then they will take it off the market. They don't have to list the ingredients used, therefore the producers of these products can simply put PROPRIETARY BLEND on the labels. That's why my dad never agreed to a product deal with his name on it, and he always said, "If you can't see it go quack, you know it's gonna be wack!"

My favorite waiter, Luis, gave me a big hug. Dad ordered his usual "Bodybuilder Lunch," a chicken breast over rotini pasta with a marinara sauce, and instructed Luis in the same way he had since I was a little girl, "So, Louie, not too much rotini, or I won't be able to fit in my posing bikini!" Luis always laughed politely and acted like it was the first time Dad had said it. I ordered the "Gold's Gym Rice Bowl" with chicken, brown rice and all the extra veggies.

It was so surreal to be there with Dad. He treated me as if nothing had changed and this was our regular Tuesday-after-the-gym lunch together. The only difference is that I felt completely uncomfortable. I hadn't actually sat in front of him in several years. I was quietly trying to think about what to talk about when he looked deeply into my eyes and said, "Bar, we need to talk!"

I smiled nervously and let him start.

"So, first, you need to know two things. One, I love you and would never do anything to hurt you and secondly, I would not let anyone else hurt you. This shit all started with Kara, my ex-girlfriend. She was very hurt that I didn't want to marry her and she told your mother a bunch of crap that simply *isn't true*. I never touched you 'inappropriately.' I have only touched you as your father, from a place of love and care. I am Italian, for Christ's sake—we touch! Your mother's family is so WASPY and uptight, I'm not sure they ever hugged one another in their entire freakin' lives."

"Dad, be nice!"

"Anyway, you are almost eighteen years old now and as an adult you can decide if your mother's request for me not to see you sticks, but I love you and I want you back in my life."

I started crying. It had been a very emotional day. I was exhausted and it wasn't even two p.m. For a split second, I wished I were back in New England, drinking hot tea with Clarissa and listening to her sensible and soothing voice. She would say, "Right, darling, it could be worse, you could be in Afghanistan, an orphan, with no, *and I do mean no,* hope for an education or an exciting life as a woman. They might even try and cut your clitoris off, for God sake."

Dad held my hand. "What is it, Bar? You can tell me anything." I looked down, embarrassed to be crying in a restaurant where so many people knew us. I waited a moment and then I just started talking. I told Dad about Miss Palmer's and the Oprichniki, why I got kicked out—which he thought was hilarious—how Mom rented out my room to a female British bodybuilder, and how utterly lost I felt. I told him about my epiphany at Gold's and that I was sure I wanted to be a personal trainer.

I wanted to tell him about my purging, but I simply couldn't.

Dad listened intently. "Bella, don't worry about it. I can help you out! To be a personal trainer, you have to graduate from high school, so you are going to have to get your GED and then take a course to get certified. You already know more than the course can teach you—you grew up with the best bodybuilders in the world, for Christ's sake—but you gotta do it for the credentials. That will take a couple of months. I'll take care of the expenses for you to get situated. You'll have to start working somewhere less competitive than Gold's. I have a crazy old friend, Maxi, that owes me a favor. He is opening a new gym on Market Street and maybe he will give you a job helping out at the front desk until you can start training.

"Also, I know you're sleeping on your mom's couch and I'd let you live with me, but I am keeping crazy hours with the show, training, and my new girlfriend, Fiona. But… I have a French-actress client that just told me she wanted a roommate for her place and it is super close to here on Dudley Avenue. She always travels and has a rich boyfriend where she spends most of her time. She just keeps the place for when she flies into town for auditions. I'll take care of the first six months' rent until you get your feet on the ground.

"Don't give your mom a hard time while I sort this out. Give me a couple of days and meet me at Gold's on Thursday around noon and I'll let you know."

Parkour
· · · · · · · · ·

WHEN DAD AND I finished lunch, he had to get to the studio for his show. I felt so full from my rice bowl I almost couldn't skate. I pulled out some candy corn from my backpack and popped several in my mouth thinking, *Why are you eating these when you are so full?* I skated down Rose Avenue to Pacific and two blocks over to Dudley Avenue to check out the apartment Dad mentioned. I went in the alley and saw a small FOR RENT sign in a window on the second floor of a cute garage apartment. That must be it. It was yellow stucco with gray trim. The location was great. It was about two blocks from the beach, a five-minute walk to Gold's, about fifteen minutes to Muscle Beach, and twenty minutes to Mom's condo on Twenty-Third Avenue.

I skated down half a block to Dudley Court and headed toward the beach. At the corner, I looked up the alley to the east and saw the perfectly framed and imposing sculptural lines of the giant Frank Gehry binoculars building on Main Street. Giggle headquarters. It was a spectacular sight, and as I was reflecting about why I loved the building so much, an extraordinary person on a skateboard flew over the horizon line down the alley racing toward me, flying past garage doors, fences, trash cans, walls, and phone poles.

It was hard for my brain to process what was going on. The first thing I got was that someone was chasing a young guy on a screaming marigold-colored skateboard, two security guards in gray uniforms...

As he raced closer toward me, I saw his beautiful and determined face. He was crouched and tucked tightly into position on his skateboard. He was lean and tan, with an unusual energy and style. He rocketed past me crossing oncoming traffic on Pacific Avenue and the two breathless uniformed rent-a-cops stopped in their tracks, huffing and puffing, watching him disappear in utter dismay.

Once on the other side of the street, the young guy hit his skateboard on the edge of a low wall on a driveway and his entire body continued to rush forward into the air as the board flipped numerous times and landed in the alley. He ran directly toward the wall of a residential garage—then ran *up* the side of the wall and flipped backwards. When he landed he continued a series of back flips, as if to say, *Try to catch me!*

He took a deep breath and charged forward again, jumped on a trash can, and effortlessly jumped onto the roof. He leapt to the main house, ran up the roofline and jumped to a neighboring house, and ran even higher. He finally arrived to the highest part of the roof facing Dudley Avenue and stopped and slowly pressed himself into a handstand. I was terrified he would fall to his death.

He lifted one arm from the roof and held the pose for several seconds before he slowly stood up, raising both arms in the air over his head, and screamed something in Russian. It sounded like "Boar-he-lick."

He laughed and ran toward the beach as if he were dancing on the rooftops in mockery. The chubby security cops turned and headed back up the alley toward the giant binoculars. One said, "Giggle doesn't pay me enough to chase guys on rooftops!"

"You got that right, brother!" the other one said, still wiping sweat off his face.

I went to retrieve the guy's skateboard in the alley. I didn't want to leave it there, and I felt sure I could find him later at the skate park. Venice was too small—if he even lived in Venice—for me not to find him. His board had a custom Element deck with a symbol I had never seen before: a red heart with angel wings. Within the heart, there was a star above, and crescent moon below. It also had something written beside it in Russian that looked like verses from a poem. I replayed the entire scene over again in my mind, how he flew over the hill, the rent-a-cops trying to catch him, his amazing acrobatics, the final handstand, and I said to myself, *I'm home!*

It was harder than I thought to skate with my backpack and carry an extra board. I hadn't skated the entire time I was at Miss Palmer's, so I felt slightly off my game. I made my way back to the Boardwalk and headed to Market Street to find Dad's friend's new gym. Maxi sounded like a mobster name. What was I getting myself into?

Once on Market Street I couldn't find a gym, or what looked like a gym, but there was one building that was big enough with two big steel front doors and a parking lot beside it. It had an old faded sign in front that read HO GROCERY COMPANY, but the building looked abandoned. There was an old homeless guy in front sitting and gently rocking on a makeshift cardboard dwelling with a distinctly Japanese Zen aesthetic. He was tall and thin, with a long salt-and-pepper beard. He looked at me silently, but didn't seem crazy or dangerous. His eyes were huge and black-brown and while his face looked exhausted and worn, there was a kindness and serenity in his gaze.

"Do you know if this is going to be a gym?"

"The sign says 'Grocery Company,'" he said with a big smile.

"Oh, yeah," I said, a little disappointed.

"But remember, darling, signs can often be deceiving!"

I smiled at him warmly and he returned the smile, and I skated back to the Boardwalk.

Just as I was about to pass Windward Plaza, I saw the parkour-skateboard guy who just escaped from the rental cops on Dudley

Court. He was running like a one-man revolution through the skate park near the beach. There was no way I could catch up with him. He seemed to be oblivious to others and used every hard surface, wall, or obstacle as an opportunity to flip, jump, or leap and run. His strength was unbelievable.

I skated to the park to ask if anyone knew him. I spoke to two guys leaning on the wall.

"Whoa, you mean Parkour Dude… that dude *claims so hard!*" the tall, lanky stoner said.

"So do you know his name, brah?"

"Well, I'm not really sure. He doesn't talk much and he has some kind of accent. He doesn't go to school. Like, if you want to *post up here*, I can try and catch up to him on my bike."

"Wow, cool, sorry, dude, I have to split. But if you talk to him, just let him know that I didn't *swoop* his board, brah."

"OK — cool. So what's your name?"

"Barbella!"

"Wow, that is a totally *bombie* name!"

I just smiled and skated over to the Windward Plaza public bathrooms.

Once alone in the humid, hot stall, I stuck my finger down my throat and tried to purge. I was having trouble and began to make a loud retching sound. I heard a little girl in the stall next to me ask her mom, "What is wrong with that girl, Mommy?" The painful part was her response, "She is just sick, honey! Like the time you ate too many hot dogs at Mary Elizabeth's birthday party."

"Will she be OK, Mommy?"

"Yes, honey, I bet she will feel better real soon!"

Maxi Ho

• • • • • • • • •

AT MOM'S PLACE, Tonya, the British bodybuilder, was standing naked on top of the center island in the kitchen. Her girlfriend, Penelope, was spraying tanner all over her chiseled body while Tonya struck poses and narrated as if she were being judged in the Miss Olympia competition.

Penelope was laughing hysterically. "Well, ladies and gentlemen, it is *very clear* that Miss Tonya has been working hard since last year's competition and we are most impressed with her improved vajazzle."

As I turned the corner to get some water, Tonya faced me. Her tanned, bald vagina was protruding and bejeweled with red, white, and blue rhinestones. She had taken so many anabolic steroids that she had actually had the beginnings of a tiny penis. Her legs were pumped and her veins appeared to be like taut cords under the skin and her large implanted breasts seemed unable to flourish under her insanely tight chest muscles. I couldn't stop looking, both in shock and fascination. It was all so wrong that it was riveting!

Tonya noticed my reaction. "Oh, Barbella, so sorry for the mess, love. We are going to register early for the Muscle Beach International competition this Saturday, and I thought I had better look my best!" Both women burst into impish laughter.

"Good luck," I said, and grabbed a bottle of water. In Mom's studio I went online and checked out what I needed to do to complete my GED and found some practice tests. The first sample question asked: Which animal has wings? (A.) Deer (B.) Dog (C.)

Hawk (D.) Snake. I thought, *Well, this shouldn't require too much preparation time. Everyone knows dogs have wings!*

I registered for the test and then looked around Mom's studio. She started designing jewelry after I left for Miss Palmer's School, so this was the first time I had a chance to see her work. It was beautiful. It looked like Mom: strong, lovely, and lyrical. She rolled silver and etched simple designs, adding sea glass, aquamarine, coral, and sea stones. I tried on some of the pieces and loved them.

It comforted me to know that my mom was interested in creating beauty and it gave me hope that one day I could find my creative voice. I was glad to know that she wasn't only concerned with her own physical beauty and men who dedicated their lives to making muscles.

• • •

By the time Dad and I met up again on Thursday, I had already completed my GED. That seemed to make him happy. We had a good time laughing about whatever happened to "Uncle Arnie" or "Uncle Franco"? Who had won what competition and who was still trying?

"Man, this stuff can get crazy," Dad, said. "We have some old-timers living out of their vans just to train and, in their mind, they still might have a chance to show the world that they have what it takes. They love to tell the tourists stories about the golden years with Arnold and the other guys."

Finally, Dad mentioned that he talked to his pal Maxi and he arranged an interview. If it went well, he would give me a job at the front desk until I got my Personal Trainer certification. He also inserted, "Bar, Maxi is a really different sort of guy and his gym is not going to be a Gold's!"

How strange could it be?

Dad also said that he spoke to his French actress client, Sophie, and she agreed to meet me to consider leasing her garage apartment for an affordable price. Affordable was important if I was going to eventually step in and pay rent on my own, and it was doubly good that working at a gym wouldn't require me to buy any new clothes.

Now that it was all happening, it felt so strange. Like in theory, I was beginning my adult life, but in reality Dad was paying for it and made it all happen. I felt determined to make it work.

"The tough part is yet to come, darling, yet to come! We shall see if you have what it takes," Dad said, as I was leaving.

When I got home, Mom was in her comfy clothes in her studio. Before I could tell her about Dad's exciting news, she told me about her "flight from hell." Apparently, one of her passengers on a trans-Pacific flight, a young female pseudo punk-rocker, insisted that her e-cigarette was technically *not smoking* and Mom had no authority to ask her to stop.

This unnerved every fiber in my Mom's being and she proceeded to club her like a baby seal with aviation safety codes: "Currently, U.S. air carriers do not allow e-cigarettes Further, it is our airline policy to prohibit use during domestic and foreign flights. If you are refusing to comply with our safety standards, *to protect you* and your fellow passengers, I will be forced to notify the air marshal and you will be detained immediately, causing a *substantial* delay in your travel plans today. How shall we precede—miss?"

When I finally share my exciting news about the apartment and the job interview, she jumped on me as if I was the girl smoking on the plane.

"I'm not very happy about your father thinking he can just show up like the great white knight and save the day, when he hasn't given me so much as fifty cents to help us out your entire life. Oh, *now* he has plenty of money to date every tramp-stamp groupie that goes to the gym and to help his daughter. I am sorry,

Bar, I would love to help you financially, but I am barely getting by myself."

"Well Mom, I'm not asking you to help me. I am sorry you've had a bad day, and you are still angry with Dad because he *cheated* on you, but have you ever thought to ask me once *how I felt*. Have you asked if I was OK? Do you think it has been easy for me? Do you think I liked being accused of being molested by my own father and then sent of to a girls prison for three years to think about it?

"Bar, I didn't send you to a prison. And of course, I care about how you feel."

"And for the record—MOM—Dad *didn't* touch me inappropriately. It was your own anger and resentment that allowed you to believe that idiot, gym slut girlfriend of his."

"Bar, watch your language."

"Watch my language? You kick me out of my own home twice and I am supposed to watch my language like I am six?"

Mom started crying. I immediately felt horrible. I touched her shoulder and asked if there was anything I could do. She asked me for a hug. I held her in my arms. I felt helpless, but I knew that I was stronger than her.

After what felt like an eternity of silence, Mom wiped her eyes and gave me her "I'm trying to be brave" smile. She reached over and held both of my hands in hers and said, "Bar I am so sorry." She began to cry again. "I have only ever tried to do what I thought was best for you. I'm sure I didn't do much right, but *you-are-so-beautiful*. I am so proud of you and I do care about how you feel. Sometimes I just get so overwhelmed, I forget to ask, and for that I am sorry."

I gave her another hug. Enough words had been said. We needed to move on. I needed to move on.

After a few emotionally awkward minutes Mom's phone ringtone went off, blaring "Stayin' Alive" by the Bee Gees. She picked it up. "Who? I'm sorry I think you have the wrong phone number. This isn't the Barbarella residence. Oh, you are trying to reach my daughter, Barbella. Just a moment please." Mom rolled her eyes and passed me the phone.

"Hello Barbarella... I am Maximilian Ho and I am Korean businessman, and a friend of your father! How are you today?"

I thought, *Did he really just call me Barberella? Wow, this guy is energetic!*

"So your daddy tells me you want to be a trainer and work at my gym!"

"Yes, sir."

"Oh please, no 'sir,' I am Maxi!"

"Sorry. Yes, Maxi, I would love to work at your gym. I am currently getting my Trainer certification and should be ready in two months, but I would love to work at the front desk until then."

"Oh, OK. I understand. First, I will interview you on the phone—OK?"

"Now?"

"Sure, why not? My world is *pali pali* style—hurry, hurry!"

"OK, I'm ready!"

"First question. How much alcohol can you handle?"

"Ahh, well, I don't really have much experience, so I would have to say not so much!"

"OK, second question. What will you do if you don't get hired by my company?"

"Hum, I will continue applying until I get a job!"

"OK, number-three question. Have you ever been in a situation where you felt you were in despair?"

"Yes, when I had to leave my family and move to Connecticut for school."

"Oh, I am sorry. Are you OK now?"

"Yes, sir!"

"Remember, no 'sir.' Just 'Maxi,' OK?"

"OK, Maxi!"

"Number-four question. How many close friends do you have?"

It was the fourth question that took my breath away. I felt a tightening in my stomach.

Do I have any close friends? There was Julie that lived next door my entire childhood. There was cousin Cassie, but I don't see her much anymore. There was Clarissa at Miss Palmer's, before she gave me up to Miss Wescott. You had better say something…

"Oh sorry, excuse me, three friends!" I said it just to say something that sounded normal.

"OK that is my interview questions. Thank you. Please come Saturday to my gym, number 54 Market Street for company orientation—OK?"

"Oh, um, Mr. Ho. I mean, Maxi. Does that mean I have the job?"

"Yeah, sure. You are now a Maxi Ho… What is that word? I always forget. Oh yeah, employee!"

"That is *great*! Thank you so much. I will do a great job and I look forward to meeting you on Saturday. Oh, and what time?"

"We shall meet at eleven a.m.—on time!"

"Yes, sir!"

"No, yes, Maxi!"

"Yes, sorry—Maxi!"

When I got off the phone, my conversation must have put Mom in a better mood. She had a huge smile and suggested that we go out to eat to celebrate my first real job.

The Ho Down

• • • • • • • • • • • • •

I WOKE UP late Saturday morning, at 10:15 a.m., and freaked out. How did that happen? I set two alarms. I ran to the bathroom and Tonya was soaking in the tub. There was a huge jar of Epsom salts next to the tube on the floor.

"Sorry, love, I'll only be a minute. I must have overdone my squats yesterday."

I headed for the kitchen and inhaled some Greek yogurt and a banana for breakfast. I was so nervous that candy corns seemed tempting, but I realized how utterly grotesque that would taste and made my way back to the bathroom and tried to ignore the fact that Tonya left her things everywhere. I didn't have time to shower so I just did a quick "French bath," threw my hair back in a ponytail, and ran to get my skateboard. I couldn't find it, so I just grabbed the Parkour Dude's board and headed for the door. By the time I hit the Boardwalk it was 10:40 a.m. and I skated quickly north toward Market Street.

When I made it to Market Street ten minutes later, I looked over toward the beach and saw Parkour Dude at the Skate Park talking to the stoner dudes that I spoke with earlier about him. The tall one saw me and pointed in my direction. Parkour stared, but didn't move. There was no way he wouldn't notice that I was skating on his screaming marigold board, but I had no time to go over and explain what happened and besides I couldn't be late to Maxi's orientation. I didn't know what to do, so I just lifted my arm in a kind of pathetic wave to acknowledge him, turned and skated toward the gym. When I looked back, he was just standing quietly with his hand on his hip, staring.

The outside of the gym still looked run down, with no new sign, and the old homeless guy with the beard and kind eyes was seated on his Zen cardboard accommodations rocking slightly. When I got to the front door he politely said, "Good morning, nice to see you again, Miss…"

"Barbella," I offered, still slightly winded from my rushed ride. He smiled. "Sometimes, Barbella, as counterintuitive as it may seem, when we are the most hurried in life, and feel the need to go the fastest, it is precisely when we need to go—the slowest!"

I laughed nervously and said, "Thanks, Plato, I'll give that some thought."

"Have you read Plato's *Symposium*?"

"No, they don't teach philosophy in high school."

"Yes, that is one part, of an ever-growing list, of the *tragedies* concerning the American educational system: they don't inspire students to inquire about the nature of love, themselves, or how they fit in the world."

"I sure like you, Plato, but I'm really late for my first day at work!"

Inside the empty cavernous space, I was greeted by Maxi from across the room. He wore a bright fuchsia silk running outfit with orange sneakers and a big roped gold chain, and stood in front of a small group of people seated on folding chairs who looked more like a band of circus performers than a commercial gym staff.

"Oh, Barbarella, my little front-desk angel—you are here!"

"Let's all give Barbarella a big applause and say hello!"

I found an empty seat beside the most beautiful African-American man I had ever seen in my life, and continued to smile as everyone gave me exaggerated applause.

"Well, if that don't make a girl feel special—I shall have to drink a cup of Dar*jeel*ing tea and ponder just what would?" my neighbor said, and smiled at me with his enormous brown-green eyes and cappuccino-colored face.

It was love at first words. He spoke with a crisp elocution that had a delicious drawl, an obvious characterization of a Southern literary poet that pulled me under his spell. Before I could get his name, Maxi called the group to order.

"OK, boys and girls, welcome to Maxi Ho Gym! First thing we do today is meet and get to know everybody."

As Maxi talked, I looked around the room and noticed there was no equipment—absolutely none. The building was bigger than it looked from the street. It was deep and had natural light streaming in from fifteen-foot-high windows across the façade. There was a large area with tatami mats. It still had a wall full of reach-in refrigeration from the building's glory days as a grocery store. "I would like you all to stand, one by one and give your name and tell us about yourself. OK, Rex, you can begin."

My beautiful neighbor sitting next to me stood unceremoniously, crossed his arms, with his right arm securing his jaw like Rodin's *Thinker*, giving his arms reason to unintentionally flex impressively. "About myself, well, I suppose by way of introduction I would like to begin with the words of my sensational Southern grandmother, Petite Savoie: 'Darling, God don't make trash and he don't make mistakes.'

"Let us contrast that remarkable sentiment with my womanizing, evangelical-preaching, Godless stepfather, Mr. Bob Peoples, *now* residing in the county jail, who would say to my mother: 'That little faggot is going *straight to hell* if one of those little idiot gangbangers don't kill him first!' And that was when he wasn't drunk and sneaking into my room forcing me to participate in *his sick shit*.

"And that would pretty much encapsulate my illustrious childhood in beautiful downtown Compton, Los Angeles. The only thing that saved me from a certain death was the tragic fact that my little sister Swish was killed innocently."

The room felt like it was filled with warm helium. I wanted to cry. The others sat motionless and completely focused on Rex.

"It was a revenge shooting for my real father, an old-school gangster who banged with the Crips in the glory days. That caused me to get really serious about my dance training.

"You see, in my neighborhood, you either joined the Crips gang, the Bloods gang, or your danced in a crew, which we called 'Clowning.' I know that sounds silly, but it wasn't, I assure you. We formed a crew and called ourselves The Crazy Eights. We were a group of tough, nay, *fierce* dancing gangsta queens that used fantasy fashion, dance, literature—especially James Baldwin and Langston Hughes—and serious weight-strength training to escape the harsh realities of our lives and kick anyone's ass that tried to bring harm to us, our friends, or our families. Now, I get to share all of my strength and training with white women who are too worried that their bottoms are too big and who can't afford a tummy tuck. I am a professional *proportionista*! Oh, and for the record, they call me Baby T-Rex back home, but don't call me 'Baby,' baby, unless you is my baby. Only my mama calls me T—so that leaves you guys with Rex!"

"OK, Baby T, that was great," Maxi said. "Now let's have the next person stand and introduce themselves, please."

Something about the way Rex communicated, with such honesty and dignity, made everyone in the room feel at ease, like it was OK to be real. Just as the next person was about to stand, the door swung open flooding in bright sunlight and Parkour Dude entered, and ran over to the group.

"Hello, Maxi, excuse me for being late, someone stole my skateboard and I had to run to work."

I nervously pushed his skateboard further under my seat.

Parkour Dude spoke with a slight Eastern European accent. Now that I was seated less than four feet away, and he wasn't running from the rent-a-cops at Giggle, I could see just how handsome he was. He had a strong angular jaw and full lips, big, dark almond-shaped eyes that seemed to tell a story of a thousand lifetimes. He was not tall, but his shoulders and chest appeared lean and powerful. His olive skin was deeply tanned. He wore four or five interesting bracelets, black baggy shorts with peace signs, and a skin-tight multi-colored tank top that appeared hand-tie-dyed.

"No problem *this time*, please seat down, Apti, and join us."

I fell into a daydream that I was in Australia, as my platypus animal spirit, swimming beside Apti. We glided effortlessly together with the sun-filtering rays of light in front of our path. There was so much warmth and serenity shared between us. My splish-splash romance fantasy was interrupted by the next trainer's introduction.

He was a solid-looking warrior of a young man with wavy, thick, red-blond hair. "My name is William Radcliff McClelland. My friends call me Halo. I got that nickname a while back when I was a Navy SEAL and I was required to jump from a helicopter on the Takur Ghar mountaintop into Afghanistan. There was unfriendly fire from the Taliban and Al-Qaeda and we had to retrieve some of our assets. HALO stands for high altitude-low opening, and I was pretty damn good at freefalling into the middle of nowhere and opening my parachute close to the ground so our enemies couldn't hear me walk in their front door. But, apparently not one night, I took a lot of grief until morning and my boys came back and got me to a hospital.

"I am lucky to be alive, and grateful to be in beautiful, sunny California. I grew up in Kansas City. I didn't want to be a farmer like my Dad. I'd never been anywhere before I joined the Navy. I fell in love with Venice Beach and I want to study acting, so I moved to Los Angeles."

Everyone applauded and Rex gave him a crisp salute. "Now isn't he a shiny penny?"

Maxi smiled warmly at Halo. "Nice to have you home and safe. You look OK to me! OK, let's have Barbarella stand and introduce herself, please."

I felt like I was naked in the lunchroom and everyone was glaring at me. I craved candy corns and wanted to run out of the building screaming. My inner voice calmly suggested, *Just tell them who you are!*

When I stood up, I stepped on the tip of the skateboard under my chair and stumbled forward. I steadied myself by throwing my hands on the back of Halo, who nearly jumped out of his seat. Everyone laughed and that gave me a moment to steady my nerves. "Right, well, as you can see, 'balance' isn't my thing! Maybe muscle balance." Everyone was looking at me so sweetly that I got even more nervous, and then my eyes locked with Parkour Dude and everything else went away. The sound of the fans turning above our heads got louder and louder until I heard Maxi gently invite me to continue.

"My name is Barbella and I grew up right here in Venice Beach. My mom and dad were both professional bodybuilders and as you can imagine I have eaten a ridiculous amount of boiled chicken, lima beans, and sweet potatoes in my childhood. I just moved back home from attending Miss Palmer's School in Farmington, Connecticut for just over three years."

Rex blurted out, "Well, all right, L'il Miss Jackie O!"

"It wasn't my first choice for my education, but ultimately it didn't matter, because they kicked me out, and that is a—*very*—long story! I am super excited to be home and working here. I am currently getting my Personal Trainer's certification." Everyone applauded.

"We are happy you came home, sweet girl!" Maxi said. "Now for our next Maxi Ho, how do you say that word? Everyone started laughing and yelled out '*Employee!*'

"Oh yes, my next employee is very special, our parkour skateboard champion, Mr. Apti!"

Apti stood up, as if in a mystical trance. "My name is Apti Murid and I am originally from Grozny, Chechnya. The so-called Chechen Republic is currently under the control—against our will—of the Russian Federation, or more clearly stated, President Putin. My life is difficult to introduce.

"In 1996, after two years of the Russian military murdering us in our homes, my father, a surgeon, took me to live in Khasavyurt, Dagestan where he worked day and night to try and bring back to life a community of displaced Chechens that fully expected to die. From there, we moved to Makhachkala on the Caspian Sea, about three hours by car to our home in Grozny. I learned parkour, or street running, when I returned to visit my grandmother for the summertime in Grozny. In the beginning, I ran from Russian tanks, through the burned-out buildings, running up walls and flipping and jumping from rooftops and then because of the bands of local fatherless boys throwing rocks at me. By the end of the summer I became a hero and a symbol for social resistance—'Bor he lick,' or 'God is great.'

"In 2011, we moved to California and I picked up skating. Now I like to mix skateboarding and parkour. I love to fly through the air. It's hard to explain in words." Apti paused, took a deep breath, and without warning began to run full speed toward Maxi. Maxi looked startled and let out a strange shrill sound. Apti effortlessly lifted himself into a front aerial walkover followed by a front flip, immediately launching into another front flip with a twist, then, facing the back of the room, he ran toward the wall. Once there, he ran up the wall and did a backflip, hitting the ground and executing another series of back handsprings, with a finale flip with a full twist. Everyone went berserk, standing and cheering. Apti seemed to appreciate the uproar and acknowledged the group with a warm, but distant smile. I noticed there was something about him—a lingering melancholy—as he made his way back to his seat.

"Now that is some *Maxi Ho* Disco Boom Boom... You can't learn *that* at Gold's Gym, people," Maxi yelled out over the group. "OK, let's quiet down!"

"I bet that boy has some real 'apti-tude,' if you know what I mean." Rex said, looking at me with a big devilish smile.

"Well, I guess I will have to be 'apti-mistic' now, won't I?"

"You know, Lil' Jackie O, I knew I liked you from the moment I saw those pouty lips and those big-ass almond-shaped jungle-green cat eyes of yours! Not to mention that thick-ass Amazon dirty blonde hair you working in an up-do!"

"People, people. Let's have some respect for our last trainer. She comes all the way from New York City. Please give a Maxi Ho welcome to Miss Vanessa Fontina." A five-foot-two platinum blonde stood up in tight white shorts, a turquoise tank top that barely kept her enormous breasts corralled, leopard-print high heels, and enormous gold hoop earrings. She wore Chanel red lipstick and was trying to conceal her chewing gum.

"So how you doing? My name is Vanessa and I'm from Bensonhurst, Brooklyn."

Rex leaned over to me and whispered, "Brick House N.Y.C.," which caused me to audibly snort out loud.

Vanessa continued, "I moved here recently from *Man*h*attan* to kick Madonna's ass, for personal reasons. Let's see... about me, so, I have a pet monitor lizard named Figaro. I just broke up with my boyfriend, who was a great-looking blond bodybuilder with a brain about the size of Figaro's. I accidentally killed my pot garden—that is, my garden is all in pots—moving to California, and I subscribe to about five hundred magazines. I have studied yoga for fifteen years. I'm not into the hot stuff, just Hatha Yoga. For me, it's about the breath. Life begins, and ends, with our breath... like when I dated a rapper named Big Bone—now that was some heavy breathing!"

Everyone laughed and Maxi tried to regain the focus of the group. "OK people, we have one more person to meet." Maxi gestured toward the door. "So, maybe some of you have met him before, but it is with great honor that I introduce to you our new Director of Maintenance and Security, Dr. Herman Feinstein."

Everyone looked around for a moment and no one appeared. We all sat quietly expecting to see big strapping guy enter the room, but no one entered. Maxi ran back over to the door and was gone for several minutes and finally, he re-appeared with the homeless man with the kind eyes from the front of the building, the one I had dubbed "Plato." He walked slowly, but with great purpose. It was obvious that he didn't really want to speak, but he would do so to honor Maxi. Maxi repeated, "Everyone, may we have a big Maxi Ho welcome for Dr. Herman Feinstein."

Of course, we all applauded with great fanfare. Plato was slow to speak.

He stood slightly swaying and silent for an awkward number of moments, looking at us all individually, with tremendous care. Although his clothes were old and faded he appeared clean. His hair was long and pulled back in a ponytail. His eyes were so large and rich with expression—spiritual—shining a loving light, as if through a stained glass.

"It is truly generous of Maximilian to extend his kindness and trust for me to lend my hand to this new endeavor. Of course, my name is Herman Feinstein, and I am not a medical doctor, nor have I played one on television. A certain person on your team has most eloquently offered me a nickname that I would *very much* like to claim as my official name here—Plato.

"She has no way of knowing how apropos and meaningful that name is for me. You see, I was a professor of philosophy at UCLA. I had a blessed childhood in Philadelphia and attended NYU to study philosophy, went on to Harvard, and finally, and with tremendous pride, received my PhD at the University of

Cambridge in England. I married a most extraordinary woman named Elizabeth, a painter with unmatched imagination and skill. When I finally reached the pinnacle of my life: high-paying job, lovely home and friends, and a terrific daughter, Hannah, the light of my life… one day they both unexpectedly left me in a car accident."

Plato stopped talking for some time before continuing with some difficulty.

"At that precise moment, I lost all desire to live, to think, or to feel. I simply walked away from 'our' home, my 'career,' my 'success,' and from the life that I had built stone by stone for over thirty years. It was all taken—in seconds. I have not worked in a very long time, so I do hope you all with be patient with me."

Plato looked down and cleared his throat.

We all felt his pain and the room was warm, as if a large blanket wrapped us together. He smiled, thanked us, and made his way gently back to the street. Everyone cheered and applauded in an attempt let him know how much we wanted to support him.

Maxi tried to lighten the mood. "OK, sexy people, time to hear the Maxi Ho, Boom Boom story…" Everyone laughed and cheered and started chanting, "Maxi, Maxi, Maxi."

"In 1970, my mother and father moved to the big city of Seoul to get rich. My mother was lucky to find a job working on 'Hooker Hill' serving cocktails. My father was not so lucky, and had to move to Los Angeles with his cousin to work. He got a job on the loading dock of Ralph Brothers Grocery store. In 1971, the Korean leader Park Chung-Hee declared martial law and my mother couldn't leave Korea.

"My father fell in love with the grocery business and my mother fell in love with a military officer, Captain 'Tricky' Lee, and in 1985—surprise—Maxi was born! Upon my birth, the nice people at the Holt Children's Services adoption agency gave me case number K85-165 and sent me to meet my *new* mommy and daddy.

BARBELLA

My new daddy was a high-ranking Korean diplomat stationed in Japan. My first spoken words were '*Watashi no okaasan wa doko desu ka?*' It means, 'Where is my mother?' They enrolled me in the Tokyo Korean School in Shinjuku.

"When I was ten years old, my father was transferred to Mexico City and we lived in an area named *La Zona Rosa*. I attended an international school and learned English. I loved the *panaderias* and the piñatas in Mexico! When I was twelve, my adopted father died and my mother and I returned to Korea. We moved to the Beverly Hills of Seoul, the Gangnam District. My mother put me in the Centennial Christian School. I hated it! By the time I was seventeen, I had dyed my hair platinum blonde and joined the pseudo-punk scene. I decided against college, or a career in manufacturing some meaningless product, and I joined a K-pop band named Boom Boom. We toured all over Korea and throughout Asia. At first, this was a very exciting life. By the time I was twenty-five years old, I had sung our big hit wonder, "Let's Make Fast Boom Boom," over ten thousand times. Every night screaming girls, every day screaming girls… I'm almost deaf! I hated being a K-pop star.

"Then my adopted mother died and I became very, very sad. I quit the band and dedicated myself to eating *bibimbap*—rice topped with meat and vegetables—all day, and drinking all night, buying everyone drinks in clubs. Soon, I became very fat, loud, and poor. After months of vomiting *bibimbap* at three a.m., a small miracle occurred and Mr. Henry Ho from America sent me a letter. He saw a music video on a Korean channel and recognized me from the photos that my biological mother had sent him. He wrote me that he was sorry for my mother's unforgivable behavior and that even though I was the son of another man, he always felt that I was his true son and invited me to visit him in Los Angeles.

"When I arrived, he lived in his small apartment in Koreatown. I slept on his old couch in the living room. He tried to teach me the grocery business, but my heart was still in music. Then, he became very ill. Before he died, he asked me for one favor. He asked me to please allow him to adopt me legally as his son. That is when I became Maximilian Ho. After he died, he left me the joy of his life—this grocery store—and a big pile of hospital bills. So, this brings me to why we are here. I have to lose some weight and make some money and I need all of you to help me!"

Everyone started clapping and making funny signature sounds. It was the most beautiful human symphony I had ever heard.

It was interrupted by Maxi screaming, "OK, Sexy Boom Boom People. Almost finished. Time to tell you about the Maxi Ho Gym!" Everyone quieted.

"So, we have a gym, this building. We have four great trainers, a receptionist/trainer-in-training, a security/maintenance man, and no equipment, no money, and no members. How can we make big Boom Boom? We must use our minds, our determination, our energy, our strength, and our hearts. When I saw a video of the parkour kids in Eastern Europe, running through bombed-out buildings, jumping off rooftops, and flipping and turning off any surface, I was inspired. I realized that the big corporations have turned exercise into something artificial.

"We must bring our members back to their natural state of human determination, energy, and strength. Everyone talks about the Paleo Diet, Mediterranean Diet, macrobiotic, organic foods but, that is simply how people use to eat naturally everyday. We will create a gym that honors what humans have done since the beginning of time—move their ass!

"We will train, and value, each member, one at a time. We will focus on natural group classes: Rex will teach a dance and movement-fitness class, Halo will teach strength and boot-camp basics, Vanessa will teach yoga, Apti will teach freestyle running and street parkour. Barbella will be the head of memberships, marketing, and the front desk. We will need everyone's ideas, help, and effort to make this work."

Rex raised his hand. "Maxi, while I adore the idea of not having a gym flooded with bad fluorescent lighting, superfluous machinery, muscle-boy wannabes, and Spandex-wearing soccer mamas running around with power bars and Diet Cokes, how do you intend to pay us if you have no money?"

"Very good question! In the beginning, the gym will function like a hair salon—we will be partners. Maxi Ho Gym will charge the member for the services and you will keep half. As you develop more clients, the share will increase. From this money, I will pay for the cost of operating the gym. As we can afford, we will make improvements and invest in any needed equipment. I have many ideas for merchandising and promotion. Does this sound OK to everybody?" Everyone smiled and applauded.

Vanessa was the next to raise her hand. "When will we open the gym?"

"Monday."

"This Monday? Today is Saturday."

"Yes! We will have a 'soft opening.' Can everyone come? Good! I will need the name of everyone's class, the times you want to teach, and what days of the week—by the end of today."

While everyone gathered together enthusiastically to chat about the names of the group classes and their unique approach to training, I saw Apti sit against the wall alone. He crossed his legs and closed his eyes as if he were going into a meditation. I took his skateboard and gently placed it in front of him. He ignored my gesture entirely.

Rejoining the others with a legal pad of lined paper, I began to make a weekly schedule. It was amazing to consider that my fingers tightly clutching this big yellow pencil belonged to the new front desk/marketing manager for a new business, one built entirely on a dream and a prayer. This large empty old building would be slowly transformed into an exciting new concept, with every trainer sharing his or her unique passion and vision. It felt like we were creating a special place for people to heal, grow, and develop. I guess from the business outsider's view we were a fairly desperate and ragged compilation of humanity, but from the inside it felt like we were something special—very special, like a phoenix rising from the sandy ashes of Venice Beach.

Home Sweet Home

• • • • • • •

IN THE MIDDLE of planning and preparing for the Maxi Ho Gym opening, it occurred to me that I had to meet my dad's friend Sophie about the apartment. I phoned the number my father had given me. I got the voicemail. A sexy voice announced, "Bonjour… You ave reached ze residanse of Sophie Charrier. I am unavailable, please leave a message." I panicked and hung up. Then I called back and left a message.

Just as I was imagining I would have to be roommates with Plato at the gym, Sophie called back. It was arranged that I would meet her and her boyfriend at a nearby coffee shop in thirty minutes to discuss the "flat," as she referred to it. I thought it was strange to meet away from the apartment, but I was so relieved to have reached her I didn't care. I explained to Maxi the necessity for my leaving, to which he said, "How do we make Boom Boom gym plan if you go?" I assured him that I would return for *big time* Boom Boom in one hour.

When I got to Groundwork Coffee Company, all I saw were two loudmouth teenage girls from New Jersey with tiny bikinis and roller skates. They were rudely demanding that the patient girl behind the counter explain each drink on the sign: *What is a Red Eye? What is a Mexican Mocha Latte? What is a Breve Latte? What is a Macchiato?* Based on their distractingly slutty appearance, they would soon be changing into county-jail orange jumpsuits or invited into the back of a surfer's van by sunset. If I hadn't been waiting for Sophie, I would have slapped them both back to the Jersey Shore.

Just as they ordered two large Mudslides (coffee extract, lowfat milk, peanut butter, banana, and chocolate, with extra chocolate sauce), Sophie walked in with her boyfriend. She was stunning. She wasn't tall, but her arms and legs appeared long and lean. Her hair was blonde, and she wore a long flowing silk scarf and beautiful golden bracelets rustling down her left arm. The boyfriend, who was introduced as Claude, was handsome and older, with thick dark hair and tan skin against a white linen sport jacket. They kissed me on the cheeks twice, ordered two espressos and then suggested that we walk outside to the Boardwalk, as the late afternoon was so lovely.

Sophie asked me about myself. And just as she asked, "Do you have a boyfriend?" at that precise moment, Apti skated within inches of me and scraped past my legs with his knees, and laughed out loud as he heard me scream. He stopped abruptly, flipping the board up to his hand like an obedient dog, and slyly said, "Thank you, Barbarella, for getting my board back to me safely!" Sophie was startled and inadvertently said, *"Merde, ce gars-là doit être fou!"* My Miss Palmer's French classes paid off. I understood what she said, "Shit, this guy must be crazy!"

Apti looked at her gently in the eyes and kindly replied, *"Un peu puisque que je vis aussi dans ce monde."* (A little because I also live in this world!)

"Wow, comment est-ce que vous parlez français." (Wow, how is it that you speak French?)

Apti seemed suddenly filled with pain and politely said, *"Ma mère. Ma mère était française."* (My mother. My mother was French.)

Sophie sensed the question was making him uncomfortable and simply said, *"Trés bien. Peut-être nous reverrons-nous dans notre appartement?"* (Very good, maybe we'll meet again in *our* apartment).

I excitedly said, "Excellent, donc j'ai l'appartement?" (Excellent, so I have the apartment?)

Sophie replied, *"Bien sur avec plaisir ma nouveau petite colocataire."* (Of course, with pleasure, my new little roommate!)

Sophie and I hugged, and I jumped around in excitement. Apti smiled warmly. "Well, it was nice to meet you both, I have to go. Thanks again, Barbella!" And just as quickly as he arrived, he departed. Claude spoke: "He seems like a very intense young man."

I agreed, and took the opportunity to ask Claude about himself. I learned that he was from French New Caledonia, which, he explained kindly, was a sovereign state of France, east of Australia in the Southern Pacific. New Caledonia had about six times the population of Venice Beach. It was a global provider of nickel, which apparently was used to make aluminum for pots and pans and high-tech products. The island had the largest protected marine reserve in the world, which covered an area three times the size of Germany. It sounded like a tropical paradise. I wanted to ask Claude if he had ever seen a platypus, but he continued talking about how he met Sophie while she was working on a French film on the island.

Sophie insisted Claude drive us to the apartment so she could go over some things with me—AC, heating, trash pickup, etc. When we entered the apartment, I was surprised how open and spacious it felt. I loved the pristine wood floors. The furniture was minimal and of nice European modern design. She had only a couple of oil paintings, but they were obviously expensive and beautiful. Gifts from Claude, I assumed. Even though it was a simple garage apartment, it felt very sophisticated.

I felt slightly uncomfortable. I worried that it was too nice for me. Even though I attended Miss Palmer's School with a multitude of rich girls, I had lived only in small claustrophobic spaces. But I was thrilled by the clean, cool, understated elegance. She opened the spare bedroom and it was beautiful, also modern, but with several stunning French antiques and more art.

She expressed her hope that I liked her taste and would be comfortable. "Well, Cherie, Claude and I have a plane to catch. I don't think I will check back here for several months because after Caledonia, I have to be in Paris for a new film. If you have any big problem, I have left how to reach me on the board in the kitchen. *Bon chance* and thank you, roomie." She gave me a big hug and departed.

I realized that we had not discussed money and quickly followed her down the narrow stairs of the apartment, "But we didn't discuss the rent and how to get you the money!" I yelled down. She laughed. "Don't worry, honey, your daddy paid me for six months already!" Claude waved to me from his Peugeot sports car and they zoomed down the alley and turned right toward LAX on Pacific Avenue.

As I went back upstairs, I must've had the biggest smile ever because a neighbor walking down the alley saw me, smiled and waved. This was going to be great. It was perfect. I wondered if Apti lived close by. The day I first saw him running from the Giggle security guards, he was only one street over.

I moved around my new apartment, enjoying opening closets, sitting on the furniture like a cozy cat, opening drawers in the modern kitchen, and discovering that Sophie had every herb and spice known to man, plus a crêpe pan. I had always wanted to make a crêpe. Then, I saw the time on the stove clock and I realized that I had been away from the gym for more than one hour. Maxi was going to kill me! I didn't know how to reach him, so I shoveled a huge handful of candy corns into my mouth and ran out. I skated full speed toward Market Street, making myself sick and feeling guilty that I had already brought my dirty little secret to my new home.

This candy corn business had to stop.

The Gang

• • • • • • • • • •

WHEN I GOT to the gym, Maxi was screaming at a paint contractor, shoving a swatch in his face. "How can you paint that color and call it this color?" The painter patiently tried to explain that the light affects the color and that the paint was wet and only the first coat. Maxi started cursing in Korean, the painter in Spanish. Maxi finished with, *"Y para su información, yo puedo entender cada palabra que me dijiste!"* ("And for your information, I understand every word you said!") The painter just shook his head and climbed up his ladder.

Maxi saw me. "You are late! Grab a brush and please start painting... these walls have to be finished today!" He turned and left the building, still cursing in Korean. I walked to where Halo, Vanessa, and Rex were painting along the big back wall. Halo was covered in red paint.

"Well, hello, Miss Mysteriously Absent," Rex said.

"Hey guys, so sorry to be late, but I am so excited! I have my first apartment!"

They all laughed and congratulated me. Vanessa asked, "So, did you get a box of condoms yet?"

Rex added, "No, baby, she doesn't need balloons. She has Sufi Rubber Band as her man!"

"What the fuck does that mean?" Vanessa snapped.

"Simply that Baby Girl has eyes for Apti and I call him Sufi Rubber Band Man, cause that boy is like a damn rubber band spinning and flipping, and he is a Sufi!"

"How do you know he is a Sufi?" Vanessa demanded.

"Well, he is from Chechnya, right? The Chechens are Muslim, so I am deducing that he is a Sufi. They are God-loving folks, and if two young person want to meet, it has to happen in a public place, and they have to sit a 'decent' distance from one another. And if it's a girl, and she has sex before marriage, Child, she risks being killed by her own relatives. I saw a show on this shit. Lord, my ass would've been dead a long time ago. So, I'm thinking that a box of condoms is supererogatory!"

"Super what?" Halo asked, obviously annoyed. "You guys are giving me a headache." Red paint streamed down his arm and all over his clothes.

"Look, Forrest Gump, if you are going to paint, try to keep the shit on the wall!"

"Oh, OK, Little Richard Wright, after you are finished with your cross-cultural analysis and suppositions on Barbella's love life—for which you know nothing—maybe you can help us paint this wall so we can actually sleep tonight!"

"Well, all right then, G.I. SEAL. Let me just remind you of a Richard Wright quote that may inspire you: 'Men can starve from a lack of self-realization as much as they can from a lack of bread. You are starting to sound *just like* Mr. Bob Peoples! Maybe if you spent more time looking within, instead of trick fucking on a hammock in the wilderness, we might actually get somewhere.'"

"I'll give you this small tip of advice Li'l Richard, it helps if you have webbed feet for trick fucking on a hammock, of course you could just use flippers, the small ones…"

"Boys, boys, boys, for Christ's sake! *All right* already! You sound like my brothers back home," Vanessa shouted. "So Bar, do you really like Apti?"

"Oh my God, I think he is adorable," I said. "Come on, I've been in an all-girls school for three years."

I heard a strange noise behind me. Someone clearing his throat, and I turned and it was Apti. After a long and embarrassing silence,

Rex said, "Well, this Moroccan Harem Red ain't gonna just paint itself on the wall. Would you like to join us?"

Apti smiled. "Sure!"

Just as we all five got into a rhythm painting, Maxi came back in screaming on the phone, in Korean, with the English words interspersed like "sound system" and a resounding closing remark: *"Tonight!"* He came over to us. "This cousin of mine is crazy. He owns a sound system company and he said we would have our system installed yesterday! How are we going to make Big Disco Boom Boom without speakers? I like this color now. It looks like hot summer night and fast Boom Boom!"

Rex paused for a moment and let Maxi walk around the room to soak in his new Moroccan red gym. "So, Maxi, what are we doing for our opening advertising? How will people know that we are open and what we offer?"

"Well, that is why I hired you! You can give me some good ideas."

"Man, we are opening in two days and you don't have a marketing plan? Even a brother from Compton knows you have to have a marketing plan!"

"No plan, just big hope. Like President Obama. Hope is powerful!"

"Well, baby, we are gonna need more than hope! We need to squeeze our ass together and get a real action plan. Barbella Baby, stop smearing red paint all over your clothes, and take some notes for me. We need to find out who can do what, pool our resources and skills together, to make a plan, and do it fast! So the first idea that comes to my mind is I can give a dance performance on the Boardwalk to attract attention," Rex barked out like a Sea captain.

Vanessa said, "I can put a straw mat down on the Boardwalk and Market, and some really tight yoga pants and a skimpy top and make a sign that says YOGA & MEDITATION CLASSES, and give the address."

"Skimpy top, and what would be different about that from today, or any day, Miss Brick House NYC?" Everyone laughed and Maxi started applauding. "Now you guys are sounding like a team—*nice* Boom Boom!"

Halo suggested that we all set up to individually take turns on the Boardwalk and promote the gym on Monday. He would wear his military fatigues and do crazy boot-camp moves, like one-arm pushups and death row rotating planks, with no shirt on, wearing his short SEAL training shorts. "Sex sells, guys!"

Apti said, "I will do some parkour moves that nobody could miss!"

I sheepishly suggested, "Guys, if we are opening on Monday, and the most foot traffic in Venice is on Sunday, don't you think we should do this tomorrow?" The reality was too obvious and everyone paused, then yelled, "Hell yea!" This got Maxi fired up and he began to sing some crazy pop song in Korean.

When everyone calmed down, I offered, "Also, that means that we have to have the class schedule complete tonight. Like—now! Rex, what are your classes called and what days and times?"

"Lord little mistress, I just don't know what to call my classes. How about, 'Snickers Ain't Helping Your Knickers' and 'White Women Can't Twerk.'" Everyone howled with laughter. "OK, seriously, let's call it 'Cardio Disco: Beginner, Intermediate, and Advanced,' Monday to Sunday. You can figure out the best times, but, Maxi, you know I gotta have that big Boom Boom sound system for my class."

"OK, Halo, what is your class called?"

Halo just kept brushing the wall, covered in red paint, with a huge concentration of paint on the front of his shirt, as if he had been stabbed in the stomach. He remained silent. Rex jabbed him. "Oh, so now I get what H-A-L-O stands for: *He Ain't Loquacious Often!*"

"Yeah, and I know what R-E-X stands for: *Ridiculously Expressive and Not Very Xenodochial.*"

"I am too nice to strangers—very nice," Rex snapped back. "*Real nice*... trick-fucking-on-a-hammock nice!"

"Right. Call my class 'Boot Camp Boogie!'"

"Oh, I like that. It is so World War II retro feeling, and has a certain Andrews Sisters vibe. Oh yeah, you gonna be our little Boogie Woogie Bugle Boy of Company B." Rex was falling over from laughing.

Maxi began screaming. "Baby Rex, if you get red paint on my clean floor, I will put you in a cage with your boogle!"

We all started laughing and in unison said, "Bugle!"

"OK, OK, people... *bugle* more paint on those walls!"

I continued trying to nail down more class names and schedules, but everyone was getting really tired and bitchy from the paint fumes.

"Vanessa, what is the name of your class?"

"'Shut the Fuck Up and Breathe Yoga,'" Rex blurted out sarcastically.

Vanessa spit back, "Yeah, that will fit nicely with your class, 'Compton Cardio: So Lil PK-Nut and Crisis Duce, from the Rollin Sixties, don't put a cap in your Harvard Park ass!'"

Everyone froze. Rex fired back a really frightening sneer. Then, in an exaggerated silly rap style, sang,

> *"Oh Lord deliver me,*
> *From this cold N.Y.C.*
> *Sista don't wanna hug*
> *She's a stone cold Yoga* thug!"

Everyone broke out laughing, including Vanessa, "All right, I know the name. Rex inspired me. I'm going call it 'Quiet Noise Yoga!'" I will offer a class whenever and to whoever wishes to take it, as long as 'Cardio Disco' and 'Boot Camp Boogie' music aren't playing in the background."

Finally, it was time for me to ask Apti and while I knew it was totally retarded of me, I felt afraid. I mean I was literally afraid of the way my voice would sound and I started worrying that he could hear my thoughts: *What if I sounded like some kind of total dork and he didn't realize that we were intended to meet? What if he could see into my brain and see that I saw us swimming together as platypuses.*

"Barbella, I am ready to give you my class name," Apti said contractually, as if annoyed that I wasn't asking him with more serious interest.

"Great" came out of my mouth involuntarily.

"I'd like to name my class 'Running from the Russians.'"

There was a pause and then Rex broke out laughing. "Or you could simply call it 'Scootin' From Putin.'"

Apti smiled. "Good one! No, I think for the American market, we shall name it 'Parkour Freedom.' And I like to teach every afternoon at three p.m. and two morning classes on Saturday and Sunday, eleven a.m. Also, you can direct people to my website, www.apti.com, or social media to see my photos and videos and learn more about parkour.

"By the way," Apti added, "I have already set up a website for the gym and some simple social media stuff. I need to improve the photos and will upload those after we do our pre-opening demo tomorrow. I had some business cards printed and designed some promotional postcards to hand out. I will have those printed by the event. What time will that be?"

Everyone just stared at Apti in disbelief. Who is this guy?

Maxi started clapping hyperactively. "Now that is the Maxi Ho Boom Boom spirit. Thank you, Apti. You are a superstar!"

Rex looked at me with his Cheshire smile. "I told you that boy had some 'apti-tude'!"

I spoke up. "Great work. Apti and I will arrive at the Boardwalk and Market by ten a.m. to hold the space. The others should arrive by eleven to set up, warm up, and get our act sorted out.

And then we can begin around noon when the folks start really moving around.

"Good idea, Barbie," Max cheered. I had an automatically adverse response to anyone that called me "Barbie" and it usually involved ax murder, but I decided to let it slide.

"Tomorrow is a big day and I want everyone to be full Disco Boom Boom!" Maxi chirped. The gang started applauding and scrambled to get their stuff and go home. "Not so fast, beautiful people! Time for Maxi Ho Gym photo shoot."

Everyone freaked out. We were tired, covered in paint, and oddly dressed. Maxi stood on the painter's ladder, like a desperate little dictator. "Please trust me. You look perfect. I have a very old friend that owes me a big favor from way back K-Pop days. A genius. I want your photos to look really raw and hungry!"

As everyone tried to get their mind around staying later, a gorgeous, super-fashion-forward Korean woman walked in wearing two cameras sporting enormous lenses, flanked by two anemic-looking assistants carrying light kits and other equipment. Maxi saw her and screamed, "Nana, you *sexy bitch*—what took you so long?" She laughed and spoke to Maxi in Korean. They hugged and discussed what he wanted for the shoot.

Maxi screamed to everyone in the room, "OK people, we gonna make *pali pali* Boom Boom photo shoot. We have one hour."

She was obviously a pro and immediately saw the opportunities in the room for optimal lighting and what she wanted from each trainer, including me. After they set up for the shoot, we all jumped, rolled, mounded, danced, pushed, pressed, split, and leapt with the last ounce of joy left in our bodies. She especially seemed to enjoy Halo. She had him take his shirt off at first, and then strip down to his underwear. Like a cat with a ball of red yarn, she teased and taunted him.

It felt like she was shooting for no time at all before Nana announced, "Great, thank you, everyone—got it! Maxi, I'll have these in your light box tonight, darling." And she was gone.

After I gathered my things and talked to Maxi for another hour, I stepped outside and took a deep, relaxing breath. The sun was beginning to set and Plato was cast in a golden light. His eyes were closed and he gently rocked forward and back with a faint whispering sound emanating from his lips. He looked different when his eyes were closed. He seemed significantly more fragile. I chose not to interrupt his meditation, and as I moved away I heard him gently say, "Good night, dear girl. Sleep with the angels!"

Apti-mistic

· · · · · · · · · · ·

IT WAS SUCH a beautiful sunset that I decided to walk up the Boardwalk fifteen blocks to visit Mom. I wanted to convince her to help me get some of my things moved tonight before my crazy work schedule started at the gym.

As I passed Muscle Beach, I heard one of the old bodybuilders I recognized from Gold's as a kid, J.T. Ketchum, schooling some skinny young men. They were obviously wide-eyed tourists. He had his hand on the tallest boy's shoulder and his other arm fully flexed. "Now son, you know how I got these twenty-two inch biceps, right? It wasn't taking steroids. They ain't surgically implanted—hell no—these muthafuckas are one-hundred-percent natural *hard working nigga*-in-the-gym biceps. That's right, every day for a year and a half I worked these bitches. I sat myself down on that bench, and I talked to 'em. Yes sir, I talked to my biceps, and as I curled I screamed 'Grow—muthafucka—grow! Every day, boys you gotta get up out that bed and make a choice, what will you be, a beast or a bitch?"

The boys seemed equal parts terrified and thrilled by his enormous vein-popping arms, covered in prison ink tattoos.

I burst out laughing, imagining him teaching a gym class at Miss Palmer's School: "OK, you spoiled little s'more-loving bitches, J.T. gonna show you just how to lose that 'Freshman Fifteen' and tighten up those little asses so you can drop it like it's hot, and freak out those little pink-dicked white boys you playing around with in the forest. I know what y'all doing!"

My coach fantasy was interrupted by commotion up ahead on the Boardwalk. I couldn't see what was going on, but there was always something going on: a fight, a performance, a movie-star sighting. I recognized a familiar pair of shorts with peace signs spinning upside down in midair and knew what the fuss was about—Apti!

As I got to the outer perimeter of the crowd I heard a boombox blasting a hot rap song by Flo Rida, I popped my head between two tall lanky guys just in time to see Apti's next tumbling pass perfectly timed to the lyrics, *"You spin my head right round, right round when you go down, when you go down, down…"*

Apti ran toward us, first doing a front aerial walkover to a roundoff, and a fast series of five back handsprings with a full layout backflip. He ended the turn with slightly split legs for dramatic effect. The crowd went wild. Next, he grabbed his skateboard and raced toward a park bench. Jumping off the skateboard, he ran onto the bench long enough to do a front aerial flip with a half-twist, placing him on the skateboard going the opposite direction. He seemed so calm when he moved, so beautiful.

I felt something I hadn't felt before as I watched him run: tension in my stomach. Not like when you eat too many candy corns or drink too much coffee—it was more like total emotional attraction filled with anxiety at the same time. It made me very uncomfortable. I thought I should leave before he saw me gawking like a total groupie.

Then, I heard something I didn't expect: the sound of someone skating quickly behind me. I secretly delighted in Apti pursuing my company. He must have seen me in the crowd. I decided to play dumb and walk faster and not turn around. Within moments, the skateboard raced up just behind me, and I felt someone grab my backpack off my shoulder and rip it off my arm.

I turned to give him a hard time, and saw that it was a complete stranger. I screamed at the top of my lungs. I'd never seen this guy. My assailant raced back in the direction of Apti, who took off running behind the guy. He snapped the backpack off the assailant's arm and kicked the guy's skateboard so hard to one side that the guy went flying and landed with a loud *thud* on the Boardwalk.

"Man, I think you fucking broke my arm," he screamed at Apti.

Apti ran back and picked up his boom box, his skateboard, a mound of unexpected money the adoring spectators left for him, and hurried to catch up with me.

"I thought I should practice before our presentation tomorrow. Shall we walk faster before the cops arrive?" We turned on South Venice Boulevard and walked silently past Strongs Drive to the Grand Canal, and walked down the ramp toward the canal.

The second I saw the water and the canal bridges, I calmed down. Apti and I walked further and stopped on the 25th Street Bridge, my favorite, with its X-patterned whitewashed wooden slats and the thick, well-worn natural wooden floorboards. We stood, side by side, quietly looking down the row of homes and little boats moored on the side of the canal.

Apti asked me if I knew why they built the canals here. I told him about the history of Venice Beach or "Venice of America," as the tobacco tycoon Abbot Kinney named it in 1905. Originally there were three miles of canals. In 1926, Venice was annexed to the City of Los Angeles and three large amusement piers were built over the water. In 1929, during the Great Depression, oil was discovered and soon there were 414 producing oil wells. They needed more roads, so they filled in most of the canals. Only six remain today. By the 1950s, Venice became known as the "slum by the sea."

He assured me that Venice was no slum, and moved closer to me on the bridge. Of course, most recently people called it "Dogtown." It was a name coined by the Zephyr surf team and the Z-Boys who revolutionized the sport of skateboarding.

"I guess in the near future, they will rename this place Giggle Beach," I said with a big smile. Apti looked at me and growled slightly. I laughed and gave a pathetic little woof in response.

We stood quietly. It was almost dark now and the lights along the canal created a dreamy, romantic quality. I started imagining him pressing his body against mine. As if he heard my thoughts, Apti put the boombox he was holding on the thick handrail. He said he needed to be able to look in all directions to spot the cops, or my assailant, if he returned. When he moved toward me, his elbow hit the boombox, causing it to drop off the bridge and plunge into the canal to its watery death.

I thought he would be angry, but instead he laughed. He lifted his arms into the air and spoke in Russian. It translated to, "What next, God? Will you take my nose?"

I didn't understand what he said, but it was so funny the way he said it that I burst out laughing and couldn't stop. That prompted Apti to move in front of my face closely and whisper, "Shhh, you will let the bad guys know we are here!" This caused me to laugh even harder and shake uncontrollably. He grabbed me gently and pushed me into his arms and put my face on his shoulder and stroked my head.

"Shhh, remember the bad guys!"

I happily surrendered to his embrace. After I stopped laughing, he redirected my face to his and kissed me gently on the lips. My mind turned into white light and our bodies felt like weightless, as if my feet would lift off the bridge and take us both stargazing. Then, I heard some little fat kid scream, "Hey, why don't you two get a room?"

We both laughed and began moving up 25th Street toward the beach. Soon we stopped talking and I could sense something strange. An energy that made me wonder if Apti was sorry he kissed me. I didn't know if I should say anything. When we got to Speedway we turned right and in two blocks we reached my mom's place.

I stopped and looked at him. "Come in, I'll introduce you to my mom!"

"Oh, I'm sorry, I can't, I have to finish my marketing materials for the gym, and, I must find a new boombox before tomorrow at eleven a.m.!"

"OK, well, I guess I'll see you tomorrow morning."

I felt so awkward. *Should I kiss him? Was that a one-time moment? Was it really a moment?* I guess Apti sensed my disappointment and grabbed my hand, and put it on his cheek. "Don't worry, be happy!" He turned and ran down the alley flipping and leaping off every available surface. Then he stopped after two blocks, turned and screamed, in Russian, "God is great!"

My mother was in the kitchen with Tonya, who was talking about training for her next competition. "Oh my God, these steroids are starting to make me look like a freakin monkey, I've got hair growing out of my bloody ears!"

"Must be all those anabolic bananas!" I said.

Mom didn't smile. "Speaking of bananas, who was that monkey flying down the alley and screaming in Russian a moment ago?"

"That is my friend from work, Apti," I said matter-of-factly.

"He seems *rather* enthusiastic. How old is Apti?"

"I don't know."

"Well, I would like to know," Mom said, as if I was guilty of a teenage crime.

"I think he's probably around twenty years old."

"I don't want him hanging out in your new apartment."

"Mother, I've lived on my own for over three years. I think I can take care of myself. He lives with his father, a surgeon. By the way, regarding my apartment, I really need your help tonight moving my stuff!"

"Oh, Bar, I am so tired. I just got home from the Singapore flight from hell. A young woman complained the entire flight to L.A. about the putrid smell of 'death and decay' coming from seat Fourteen C, the seat in front of her, insisting that it must be the anus of Satan. Can't this wait until tomorrow? Why don't you get your heroic father and his slutty girlfriend to help you?"

"Mom, how do you know she is a slut?"

"*They all are,* darling, trust me!"

"Dad is probably working late on his show. Come on, Mom, I really need your help. I have to work tomorrow, and we have a promo at ten a.m. on the Boardwalk. Please, please—*please* Mom!"

"OK, but I want to talk some more about this Apti fellow. What kind of name is Apti?"

"Chechen."

"Where is that?"

"In Russia."

"Is he a Communist?"

"No!"

"Oh God, my daughter is dating a Chechen *terrorist!*"

Trouble in Dogtown

• • • • • • • • • •

MOM AND TONYA helped me move my stuff to the new apartment, and we had a nice dinner a couple of blocks away, at the Figtree Café. They continued to grill me about everything: my job, the gym, the other trainers, and of course, Apti. I felt so grown up, going to dinner with Mom. It was a really nice evening until Mom and I heard a woman screaming bloody murder in the ladies' room. Apparently she thought Tonya was a man and freaked out. Tonya just laughed it off and told us it happened all the time.

Before I fell asleep, I thought about Apti. I played back how he rescued me on the boardwalk, our unexpected kiss on the bridge, and how he pulled back afterward. But then he left with such an energetic departure. *And what is "Don't worry be happy" supposed to mean?* After my first failed romance back at Miss Palmer's, I was starting to feel a bit confused. And maybe, underlying that, I felt afraid.

The next morning, I decided not to figure out Sophie's fancy French coffee maker just yet. I dressed quickly, skated to Groundwork for coffee, and continued to the promo spot for the gym on the boardwalk at Market Street. There really wasn't anyone around so it was easy to reserve our performance space. The Venice Sidewalk Market wasn't yet hawking cheap shoes, Chinese foot massage, or knockoff designer sunglasses.

Looking up Market Street two blocks, I could see Maxi's building, but two commercial parking lots' activities interrupted the view. An enormous mural ran the distance on the side of Maxi's building, front-to-back visible from the Boardwalk. Sadly, gangs had tagged the entire thing, making for an untidy visual soup: dissonant colors, shapes, and unreadable, stylized graffiti. At the highest part of the wall I could pick out the only clear images: a silhouette of a blonde bombshell with sunglasses, a deranged-looking bearded guy, a young Native American woman with a hard glare, an older African American woman with a pensive gaze, and an Aztec deity, Ometecuhtli ("Two-Lord") representing the opposing forces in the Aztec universe: male and female, light and dark, motion and stillness, and order and chaos.

I made a mental note to tell Maxi that we needed to paint over the mural and create some signage for the gym. As if by a miracle or some prayer answered by Lord Ometecuhtli, two old vans with huge ladders pulled up to the gym with LEE COMMERCIAL PAINT COMPANY in big red letters. Maxi walked outside and talked to them, pointing and gesturing.

Just at that moment, one of the Venice Beach legends arrived on a unicycle in a leopard loincloth. He held two long plastic snakes and a cane pole. He wheeled straight for me, speaking in some kind of fake African gibberish and aiming his snakes at me in an apparent effort to scare me. I skated a couple of feet out of his path and he turned straight for me. After yesterday's attack, I wasn't in the mood to be messed with and my old Venice Beach swagger was coming back strong.

I stepped straight toward him. "What *the hell* are you doing?"

"I am coming to work, baby girl! *And you* are standing on *my corner*."

"Well, that is just a funny coincidence, because I too am coming to work, and since I am here first, this is clearly *my corner!*"

"Little girl, you have nothing to do on this corner. I, on the other hand, am a professional entertainer. I have performed on this very corner for royalty, Hollywood stars, and damn near everyone else from Poughkeepsie to Portland!"

"Well then, surely your presence will be equally appreciated one block further in either direction!"

King Mamba got off his unicycle, stood on top of his brightly colored plastic bucket, rattled the bells around his ankles, and pulled out the orange plastic flute stuck on the side of his loincloth. He played a loud, furious tweet. He then spoke again in his fake African dialect shouting, "Oh Lord, Mabumba kundalini martini and Mista Ho—please help me to get this girl to know that *this is my corner!*"

"So King Mamba, did I hear you say 'Mista Ho' as in, Mr. Ho *from* Ho Groceries?"

"We are standing steps from Mr. Ho's grocery, Little Miss!"

"You know Maxi?"

"Oh hell yeah. Mista Henry Ho, that boy's father, lived here most of my life. He was a living and breathing saint!"

"You knew his dad well?"

King Mamba got off the bucket and lowered his snakes. "He practically raised me when I was wild boy on the streets from Oakwood. We was so poor, my house didn't even have a damn foundation. And at twelve years old, ain't nobody, and I do mean *nobody,* gave a shit about little ole me, except Mr. Ho at the grocery store. Always helping me with my homework, making sure I had something to eat, or a warm place to sleep when my father started acting a drunken fool. I truly loved that man."

"Well, sir, I am here today because Maxi is opening a new business tomorrow and we are trying to promote it today—here—so we can direct folks over—there—to the new gym."

"Maxi? Little chubby Maxi gonna open a gym? What is he gonna called it?"

"Ho gym."

"Oh Lord, my kinda gym!"

I could hear someone behind me say, "No my friend, a gym that values human life. No muscle gorillas on steroids. One hundred percent natural." I turned and saw Apti, looking adorable in baggy gray shorts, red mesh running shoes, and a black t-shirt with a huge white peace sign.

"A Natural Ho… I like that! Plus, it's good for ya!" King Mamba gathered up his stuff, still laughing, and offered up a friendly parting comment: "All right, children. Just remember this truth. Mista Ho use to tell me, 'What waits for you ahead is *always* better than what you left behind, don't be afraid to take the journey!'"

I smiled. "I sure hope so!"

Apti gave me a big hug and a nice smile. He looked a little tired, explaining that he had stayed up all night finishing up the gym-promo postcards and dropping in the new images from Nana's shoot for the website and social media, and he had to get up super early to have them printed.

It seemed strange that Maxi would call him so late. *Is that why he pulled back? Is he gay?* I just had to find out, "How long have you known Maxi?"

"I've known him since he came to L.A."

"How did you meet him?"

"His father and I were close. When my father and I arrived to Venice, we barely had enough money to live and we didn't speak English."

"But I thought your father was a surgeon?"

"Yes, but he hadn't passed the medical exams in the United States and therefore couldn't practice medicine! To pass the exams, he had to learn English first. In Chechnya, we didn't find a great deal of use for English. The Russians were too busy trying to kill us. I learned English by listening to rap music with an English dictionary. That was funny. Can you please translate for this Chechen boy, '*Drop it like its hot Li'l Boo, cause baby you know I'm the nigga dat love you*'?

"Of course, most of the slang made it difficult to really learn how to speak correctly. It caused some strange looks and embarrassing moments when I first arrived. For example, I thought, 'What's up, baby?' was as common a greeting as 'Good afternoon, how are you?'

"Anyway, one day I was so hungry after running I stole some bread from Maxi's father. He caught me, but he didn't call the police. He handed me a broom and said, 'You hungry... you no steal from me, you work for me."

"Jesus, is there anyone that Maxi's dad didn't help?" I said, laughing.

We were both startled by a sudden deep voice, "Excuse, my friends, is this what the locals refer to as Dogtown? 'Cause if it is, I'm bout to tear this shit up with my dirty dog dancing."

We laughed and hugged Rex. I looked up Market Street and was shocked to see that the paint crew had already sprayed on a white coat of primer over the mural. Even though graffiti tags trampled the old mural, at least they gave the building some human life and modern character.

We heard Halo approaching us, looking very G.I. Joe-sexy in short—very short—UDT khaki trunks and a belt, a skintight plain white t-shirt, black combat boots with the socks rolled over the top, and a floppy camouflage Boonie hat. He was belting out a Navy cadence as he marched down the Boardwalk: *"I don't know but I been told... Muscle Beach is for the old... sound off one-two... I don't know but I been told, Gold's Gym smells like stinky mold... sound off three-four... I don't know but I been told... Maxi Ho Gym straight-up gold..."* We all joined in for the last chorus of *"sound-off one-two-three-four,"* and greeted our colleague with laughs and high fives.

Shortly after Halo's arrival, Vanessa came from Market Street, swinging her hips and clacking up the Boardwalk in black Christian Louboutin stiletto heels, tiny white yoga pants and a low-cut baby-blue leopard leotard, with a stunning blue silk Hermès scarf with a circular sundial motif. It gave her a sense of importance and presence. "Oh my God, I'm gonna turn into a freakin lobsta out here," she said. "Who has the sunblock? Are you guys trying to kill me? The last time I saw this much sun and sand, I got the crabs on the Jersey Shore with my weekend *colpo di fulmine* named Victor!"

I could see Maxi in the distance receiving yet more service trucks and vans, and the building was teeming with activity. "What the hell is Maxi doing?" I muttered.

The gang all said in unison, "Making *pali pali* Boom Boom!" Just as I was about to admit that I had absolutely no clue what to do for today's "gym promotion," Apti stepped forward. "OK, I have the promotional postcards for the gym. As you will see, I have used all of our images from the photo shoot yesterday with Nana." Everyone crowded in closely as he made a manual slideshow of the different cards and the images. The overall consensus—wow!

The images really brought out the strength and vitality of each trainer, and the art direction was super fresh and interesting—especially with all that red paint over everyone and the gritty honesty of our look. The headline was the same on all the cards: HO GYM STATE OF MIND, and below that, 100% NATURAL. They were great! Apti suggested that I hand them out to the crowd as each trainer gave a ten-minute demo class.

We decided that Vanessa should begin in a meditation pose and then do a series of sun salutations. Apti put on some awesome hypnotic flute music. As I watched Vanessa, bathed in light, the music filled me with tremendous emotion. It was the contrast of how happy and at peace she appeared, and how afraid and unresolved I felt.

I envisioned myself throwing up at my mom's old apartment and at Miss Palmer's School. I was tied up in knots, and didn't want anyone to notice. The music filled me with emotion about my childhood. I felt sad and didn't know why. And then it hit me. My God, it was a contemporary remix of the music from when I was a little girl at my babysitter's, Mama DeySarkar's house. It was the Indian flautist, Hariprasad.

The emotions pushed me over the edge. I gave the promo cards to Apti and whispered, "I've got to go to the bathroom, and I'll be *right back!*"

I ran as fast as I could for two blocks to the gym. Inside, Maxi was arguing with a small group of Korean contractors and didn't see me run to the ladies' restroom in back. I shut and locked the door, sat on the toilet, and cried my heart out, as quietly as possible.

After five minutes, *I thought, I've got to get it together. Those guys are depending on me.* I stuck my finger deeply down my throat and choked violently. Then I washed my face with cold water and realized there were no hand towels. I wiped my face on my t-shirt and quickly made my way to the door. To my surprise, Plato was standing there. He turned to face me with a loving, yet troubled look in his eyes. I know he heard me. I wanted to throw myself into his arms and continue to cry, but instead I manufactured enthusiasm. "It's really going great out there!"

Plato stood calmly in the doorway, gently swaying, and looked deeply into my eyes for a long time.

"When we are about to have real and significant changes in our life, true growth takes on many strange forms," he said. "Sometimes it can look like aloneness, pain, and chaos, but these are simply illusions. Emotional cloudbursts, momentarily distracting us, blocking our ability to see the love of God, that is always present and available to help us heal our pain."

"Plato, that is some *deep shit,* my friend!"

"The deepest, little one, the deepest."

He moved to one side and allowed me to pass.

• • •

As I slowly walked back to the Boardwalk, I noticed an unusual amount of young African Americans gathering at Windward Plaza.

Not the usual small groups of friends that you always see on the Boardwalk. There was a sense that something was going to happen, yet the crowd was not facing any one direction, or organized. I saw the gym gang doing the promotion on the Boardwalk and people were stopping and taking the cards, which made me feel great. As I got closer, I noticed Rex was dancing and several young men were throwing bad attitude at him. He seemed to laugh it off and danced even harder. I'd never seen him move and I was blown away by how fluid, strong, and precise he danced.

I noticed the other trainers getting nervous and moving closer to the young hecklers. By the time I got close enough to hear, Rex was moving rapidly toward the young men and Apti had turned off the music.

One of the young men pushed up to Rex.

"Look, man, I know you out here trying to pimp dem hoes, but you are fucking wit my business here today, you feel me? You see, I am a straight up Ghost Town nigga. My people been here a long time. Yeah, oil-patch niggas gone Crip, which means you got to get your oreo nigga ass off my boardwalk. You understand what I'm saying?"

Rex stepped up and put his face squarely in the face of the young man. He looked deeply into the young man's eyes and was silent.

"Man, what the fuck? You trying to punk me, nigga?"

Rex leaned in further. "Oh, so you is a Oakwood Crip nigga… now that is *some kind of special*."

"Yeah, ghetto-by-the-sea nigga." The young man lifted his shirt, exposing a pistol tucked into his jeans. Rex didn't hesitate. He pushed right up against the boy's chest with his.

"Oh, represent my young nigga, now that is something. What a coincidence. Cause I'm a stand-up nigga from Harvard Park Brims, Rollin Sixties. You know what I'm saying, I'm an OG mutha fucka and my Uncle Tookie wouldn't even talk to your Oakwood punk ass. So you wanna fuck with this South Central clownin nigga? I'll show you some real G shit!"

The boy backed up and his rigid body softened. "What? Tookie is your uncle? Damn brother, my bad. I didn't mean any disrespect; you know what I'm saying? Look G, me and my partners wish you well—ain't no problem here today, my brother. We out!"

"Yeah, all right then!" Rex pulled back from the young man. Everyone let out a big sigh. Rex stood silently for a long moment staring at the young men walking into the crowd.

"Wow, I am sorry you had to experience that. It breaks my heart that we spend almost six hundred billion dollars annually on our military in this country and our kids are still struggling to get an education and out of poverty. Believe me, 'We the people' *truly understand* the meaning of 'In God We Trust!'"

"Rex, look at it on the bright side. You got out. Maybe you could give those kids a class for free and help them get off the street!" Vanessa said.

"Actually, that might be a very good idea, Vanessa," Rex said. "You know all those boys just want the love of a father. Lord have mercy, let me stop, before I start crying and preaching."

Everyone agreed it would be a good idea to take a lunch break and regain our excitement and focus. We noticed that more young people had gathered in Windward Park, especially around the basketball courts.

"Guys, something is wrong," Rex said. "Those kids' aggressive attitude, the huge number of kids gathering at this *specific* location, all these cops starting to arrive. Many of these young folk are wearing gang colors and it isn't just the Crips from this area. I recognize some of them as Bloods, and it is *very* unusual to have the two mix."

Before Rex could get his next sentence out, we heard multiple gunshots ring out. There were screams, followed by panic, and kids scattering in all directions.

We all ran toward the gym. Vanessa lost a heel on her shoe and could be heard screaming, *"motherfucker"* above the mayhem of the crowd. She couldn't run on one stiletto heel, so Halo swooped her up and ran with her as if she were a big-breasted, bouncing blonde teddy bear.

Outside the gym entrance, Maxi looked worried. He was waving his arms for us to hurry. *"Pali pali,* people!" Somehow the familiarity of his voice made me feel calmer. I had lived in Venice my entire life and had never experienced something like that. I saw stuff on the news in the bad neighborhoods all the time, but it was really different when you are in the middle of it in broad daylight in a major tourist area and hear gunshots. It was *really* frightening.

Maxi seemed agitated. A lot of Korean businesses had been looted and vandalized in the L.A. riots in 1992. Rex assured Maxi this was different, not a riot. This was probably some kid tweeting out a flash-mob gathering to Crips and Bloods to meet and "represent." Maxi didn't understand what a "flash mob" was, so we explained that is was simply a digital message on your phone that says, *Hey everybody, meet at this location, at this time, for this purpose.* Rex reminded us that revenge shootings were common among gangs. That was why his little sister, Swish, was murdered. It could go back generations.

Maxi said, "I am so happy that my Boom Boom Super Team is OK!"

"OK, what about my freakin five-hundred-dollar shoe!" Vanessa cried.

"Calm down Runway N.Y.C., you know damn well those Chinese knockoffs didn't cost you five hundred dollars."

"Rex, you wouldn't know an Armani from a Phil-harmoni." Vanessa retorted.

"Baby, don't *ever* underestimate the cultural clowning of a Compton connoisseur!"

We could still hear a lot of noise coming from the street. Halo went outside and flagged down a cop, who told him that an African American male had been shot on Seventeenth and Speedway. My stomach hurt. It was only six blocks from my mother's house.

Halo reported that young people were still running down the Boardwalk, LAPD uniforms were on almost every corner, and two police helicopters flew overhead. Vanessa said, "Maybe we should pass out promo cards to the cops. I bet they could use some yoga and meditation right about now."

Apti became agitated and put his head down. He tried not to show it, but we could feel his emotional tension. Halo looked at him and gently said, "What's up, brother?"

Apti lifted his head and it was obvious he was holding back tears. "This brings back bad memories... very bad memories. In Chechnya—since I was born—the Russians have killed one hundred and sixty *thousand* people, including my mother, my sister, uncle, and four cousins. Yet, *we are the ones the world calls the terrorists.*"

Halo put his arm around Apti and squeezed him. "We got you, brother. We got your back."

I wanted to hug Apti. Instead, I excused myself and went to the ladies' room.

Ho Gym

● ● ● ● ● ● ● ● ●

MAXI PROUDLY SUGGESTED that he give us a tour of the gym and show us what he and his crews were able to accomplish *"pali pali* style" since we all gathered last night. To our utter amazement, the gorgeous photos from Nana's shoot were mounted and hung on the Moroccan Harem Red walls. The images were bold and stunning in the space. The new *tatami* mat floors in the yoga/meditation area were installed, with a large glass partition that caused Vanessa to shriek, "Oh my God, this is a freakin' soundproof sanctuary. I love it!"

In the back of the building, Maxi had converted his father's old apartment into a small living space for Plato, who to date was still more comfortable rocking in front of the gym. We found a strange drawing on the small dining table. Halo picked it up and said, "Hey, Maxi, looks like one of the construction worker's kid did an art project for you."

It was a very primitive drawing on paper that looked like a crude illustration of an African American trumpet player wearing a large crown suspended over his head. Then the words SAMO Sachmo written several times and SAMO was scratched out.

"That child should consider a new career... Art classes are not working! He and his family will *starve* to death. What does SAMO mean in Spanish?" Maxi said, as he wadded the drawing into a ball and threw it in the trash can.

"Maxi, don't be so hard on the kid," Halo said, as if he were the father.

"Sir, you seem to be interrupting the tour, please continue," Rex instructed.

"Come on, move your ass!" Vanessa snapped at Rex.

"I'll show you move, Miss Brick House, N.Y.C." Rex responded with a smile.

"OK people, let's continue the Ho Gym tour, please," Maxi said, like a father herding baby ducks into a pond. The big surprise was the addition of two complementary businesses in the back of the gym. A juice and snack bar that he called "Juicy" and on the other side of the warehouse, a massage spa that he named "Yo Spa."

"Yo Maxi, why would you name a spa "Yo?" Rex asked, trying to be respectful but obviously disapproving.

"In Korea, the dragon that lives in the ocean is called Yo. This dragon is very kind and protects the country, and can bring rain for the farmers. Yo is a symbol of good luck."

"Fabulous, Maxi. You know that *yo* means 'I' in Spanish, right? So now our members will say, 'Yo, want to go to the Juicy in the HO — that is really poetic!" Rex said.

"Or, you can skip the Yo part, and go straight for the Juicy Ho…" Halo responded.

"Or you can just *come* in the Ho!" I said, without thinking.

Everyone busted out laughing, except Apti. After I realized what I said, I turned as red as the Red Harem walls. Apti gave me a disapproving look, and I felt embarrassed.

"OK naughty children, time to have a *talk*. First, I want to thank you for all that you have done to make Maxi Ho Gym a reality. Sorry your boardwalk promo was stopped by crazy *Gangpae*. You work hard and I like that, good *Boom Boom* everybody — thank you!"

"Maxi, you did all this work in the last forty-eight hours? How did you get permits so fast?" Rex asked, sincerely.

"God helps those who help themselves — right?" Maxi smiled like a naughty boy stealing a cookie. "Now, about tomorrow…

Barbella, do we have the schedule ready? Guys, do you know what time you need to be here? Do you have your classes ready? Apti, do we have a schedule on the new website? Are you ready to describe each class, Barbella, when people visit the gym, or call? Wait a minute… when they *call?* Big, big, problem people, Maxi forgot to get a phone number for the gym!"

"What? You don't have a phone number?"

Maxi laughed. "I was so busy, I forgot!" That caused everyone to break out laughing.

"It's OK, you can use my mobile phone number until you get one," Rex offered.

"Oh, thank you, Baby Rex!"

One of the guys on the paint crew walked in. "Mr. Ho, we have the building painted and the lettering done on the side wall."

We all ran outside, excited to see the new look of the building. It was hot orange-red. On the front, it read HO GYM and on the side facing the Boardwalk, but in letters about ten feet tall — HO GYM, and below it 100% NATURAL.

Rex said, "Well, ain't no mistaking what goes on up in here!"

Three

Snapshot: Two Months Later

• • • • • • • • • • • • •

IT WOULD BE GREAT to report that Ho Gym is thriving, I am a trainer, and that Apti and I spend all our time together in rapture. The sad reality is none of the above is true.

The gym is struggling and Maxi is stressed out, which stresses me out—and increases my candy-corn consumption—and it is difficult to act excited about selling the memberships when tourists walk in the door *daily* and ask if we *really train whores* at Ho Gym. Which usually prompts me to say, "Why not? They have to be in shape as much as anyone else!"

The Venice Beach locals ask things like: Do we have a steam room? Do we provide towels and is yoga included in the membership? What does 100% NATURAL mean and *why is that desirable?* What does *parkour* mean? Why don't we have free weights, elliptical machines, and showers?

Not to mention the challenges of the members that we do have. Let's just say they are a *very unique* group. Like, Mr. Litton, age eighty-two, tall, tan, lanky, an ex-Hollywood stunt man who wears tiny white gym shorts and no underwear, allowing his fat old warbler to fly around freely as he rolls around the mats doing stretches. Vanessa refers to him as "Puff the Magic Dragon." You can often hear Rex walking around the gym, while Mr. Litton is working out, singing, *"Puff, the magic dragon lived by the sea, and frolicked in the steamy mist, in a land called Venice Beach…"*

All of the trainers seem to be hanging on, either because of existing clients they brought with them, or new clients they've been able to find. Rex has had the most success because he goes to the one local gay bar, RoosterCock, which is open seven days a week. He dances to meet people, and then passes out cards. It is hard to watch Rex dance and not want to move; he's gorgeous and expresses himself like a sinful prayer.

Rex's biggest success has been his Thursday night freestyle retro-disco class that he simply calls, "Booty Swang." He packs the place with horny fifty-year-olds that want to move their groove thang. Halo loves to mess with Rex about how many "cougars" he attracts to his class. Trust me, this is something to behold. From dancing the "bump" to freestyle arms swinging in the air and hips gyrating, these old girls get frisky. Even though Rex is obviously gay and half their age, they dance with him like he is their pet panther. Rex just smiles that Cheshire smile and slaps them on the ass with stinging conviction and says, "Work it, baby!"

Vanessa fills her Sunday afternoon yoga class to capacity. It seems to be some kind of alternative church experience for many of the members and it attracts some curious birds. Like the woman Rex calls "Cousin It," as in from *The Addams Family*, because she has hair down to her ankles. She puts it up for class, but it falls down at least five times during downward dogs, giving her the combined appearance of an Afghan hound and a longhaired guinea pig.

And of course, Vanessa has devout followers, like the pencil-thin blonde that looks like an anorexic young Joni Mitchell and refers to herself as "C. Kevin." It took four visits for me to realize that she had changed her name to reflect her ambition to "seek heaven."

The most alarming Sunday yoga visitors were the women in their late twenties or early thirties who illegally parked next to the building in their Range Rovers. They were *always* late and came to class wearing large diamond-stud earrings, their engagement rings, usually a two-carat fancy yellow cushion-cut diamond, with perfectly manicured hands and toes, designer yoga outfit and full make-up. And then there's Tonya, Mom's roommate, and her female bodybuilder friends, who come to work on their flexibility. Rex refers to them simply as "English T and her Muscle Beach Crumpets!"

Apti, what can I say about that boy? He is amazing. I rarely see him because I am always working or studying for my trainer certification. But when he comes to the gym, everything feels different: the energy of the room, my mood, and the way people respond to him. He doesn't really hang out with the trainers at the front desk. Most of his clients are young, and their parents bring them in because their kids found his blog, or saw his videos online, and they absolutely freak out over how cool and amazing he is in his sport.

Apti takes the kids over to the Venice Beach Skate Park and when they come back, they beam with excitement and put his arm around their shoulders as if he were their sacred big brother.

His sense of humor comes from a very different place than the other trainers, deeply ironic and intellectual. The kind of humor that is distinctly cultivated from another culture, a mind that truly knows itself prematurely — an old soul — and speaks as if God is in the room.

When he is around me, he is polite and funny. He seems attracted to me, but doesn't ask me out. I haven't been alone with him since he kissed me on the bridge. I know he is very spiritual and from what I read online about his culture, we are from two opposite sides of the world, but why does he keep a quiet distance between us?

Halo has hustled a lot of private one-on-one sessions. His group class "Boot Camp Boogie" tends to have an exceedingly high burnout rate. On more than one occasion, he has made women and big men cry. Halo hasn't learned how to moderate the intensity level of his class and he works them like they are literally going to war. Most folks romanticized the idea of being as fit as a SEAL, ready for combat and all that. But they had no idea what they were getting themselves into training with an ex-killing machine. Most members don't want to do seventy pushups in just less than two minutes while someone screams insults at them!

One of the worst moments at the gym occurred when Rex and I were at the front desk and met with a girl named Nancy, a super-shy high-school freshman, and her ex-military officer father, Captain Wessman. He was tall, and stood very straight.

"I understand that you have a trainer here that was a Navy SEAL, is that correct?"

"Yes, Mr. Wessman, you are referring to Halo," I said sweetly.

"That's Captain Wessman, dear, and Halo is not a name," he responded acidly.

"Well, sir, I mean Captain Wessman, his name is William McClelland, but we all call him Halo."

"I need McClelland to whip her fat ass into shape by the end of summer or I'm going to send her to Arizona to a fat farm," he said with a chuckle. "Her ass was an unfortunate gift from her mother, who never seems to get off hers to do any exercise."

I could feel Rex getting agitated. Because his stepfather abused him for so many years, he had a very short fuse around tyrannical assholes. I didn't even look his direction, and secretly prayed that he didn't engage him in conversation.

Just as I was going to ask the Captain when they might like to begin, Rex leaned in and asked him, "So, Mr. Wessman, if your wife had such an *unfortunate* disposition, why did you choose to marry?"

"My name is *Captain* Wessman—*son*—and my personal affairs are none of your damn business!"

"Well, *Captain* Wessman, since you are the one *giving us* personal business about your wife, and as we don't have barracks in the gym, and I'm *clearly a 'tell'* and you *don't have to ask* sort of *gay man*—I think—I will just call you Bob!"

And with that, Rex lifted his right arm up high and began to recite a prayer: "Oh Lord grant me serenity to accept the things I can't change, courage to the change the things I can, and the wisdom to know the difference," and quietly walked out of sight.

The Captain gave Rex a long, hard stare. "Hope McClelland has more manners than *that*... I want her to get started today."

Nancy's knees buckled under the weight of her father's hideous remarks. After he left her for her first session with Halo, she fell apart and ran directly to the ladies' locker room and wouldn't come out. She was crying so loud that Plato heard her and came to tell me. I tried to comfort her, but her father's comments had cut too deep to stop the bleeding.

I talked to Halo about what her dad was putting her through and he agreed to take her on as a special project. He swore to me that he would be a loving and patient trainer.

Nancy would be a welcome and worthwhile place to focus his attention, in lieu of the countless men and women that hired him simply to try to seduce him sexually. I never really found Halo that attractive. I did love his strawberry blond hair, his rugged body, and the intensity of his emerald green eyes, but he struck me as the kind of guy that looked for someone to go wilderness camping with in the backcountry of Alaska. I imagined that they would build their own shelter from tree trunks and limbs, hunt for dinner with bow and arrow, bathe naked in the freezing streams, and only talk about the serious survival matters at hand—sex in the tent! After having personally experienced dating under a baby grand piano, in my mind, luxury and a comfy bed was key.

As for other parts of the gym, Juicy, the snack bar, seems to do well around the lunch hour, but the profits barely cover its costs.

It seems fairly popular with the young Giggle guys that like to sit for hours, not spending money but writing code over coffee or a small cold-pressed juice.

The YO Spa also seems to be popular with the Giggle guys, especially when they need to knock the edge off, so to speak. Maxi hired several Korean women as "massage therapists." I am not sure they have ever been officially certified, but I imagine most of our male members received a complimentary "happy ending" and therefore didn't really care about their therapists' credentials. Maxi found these women through his biological mother who had recently reconnected with him, after thirty years, at Mr. Ho's funeral. Apparently she has the contacts from her days on Hooker Hill to supply beautiful, professional "massage ladies" who are more than happy to live in Los Angeles.

In spite of our minor business successes, the overhead expenses are killing us and each month is a struggle to keep the gym doors open. Maxi is becoming more desperate for fast moneymaking schemes. Daily, he comes in wearing his orange velour workout outfit with a fuchsia t-shirt, thick gold chain, and his two pug dogs, Pinche and Puto, and discusses his latest ideas.

The first involved trying to attract young Hollywood actors to the gym, a project he called, the "Hollywood Ho Down." Sounds reasonable, right? Venice has some famous actors that call the canals home and the young up-and-coming starlets are frequently seen on the Boardwalk. After all, our gym is only one hour and fifteen minutes by car from Paramount Pictures. The big question was if these Hollywood folks would travel to Venice to work out at our gym? In my childhood, I had seen countless stars training at Gold's with my dad, but that was a different time. Americans didn't know much about fitness training back then and there wasn't as much traffic on the roads.

Maxi gathered all the trainers and announced, "People, we need some more Hollywood customers to Boom Boom at the gym! We need to make Hollywood Ho Down."

"In my experience, including with Hollywood, men are willing to travel. Believe me, Maxi, they will travel if you give them a compelling reason!" Vanessa assured Maxi.

"Amen, sista, if you serve enough chip and dip, baby, a man will fly to find ya and then cross the desert just to get next to your *sphinx*" Rex said laughing and adding a little Egyptian dance move.

"What the hell does that mean?" Halo blurted out, scratching and shaking his head.

"Nothing your caveman ass would comprehend."

"You're right, I wouldn't comprehend a man flying to see me, and walking across a desert to get next to my 'sphinx.'"

"*Children*—focus—this is serious stuff," I said trying to steer the guys into a serious discussion.

Maxi's scheme does have some logic. The obvious reason for any actor to visit a gym is to either lose or gain weight. Further, Venice Beach is a location constantly frequented by paparazzi trying to spot actors, and someone is always getting 'papped' for looking too fat, drunk, or some other stupid reason."

"Baby Bar, we should shoot some fake celebrity shots of actors walking into the Ho Gym, and then we could post them on social media. If folks in Hollywood thought that Ho Gym was the new "it place," those over-pimped Botox beauties would be coming in here in waves. Problem solved!" Rex smiled, amused by his own idea.

Rex had a good point. We just needed to plant a seed. As per usual, Maxi, with *pali pali* speed, found Angelina Jolie and Matt Damon lookalikes, and convinced Nana to come back one more time to shoot our doppelganger models entering the Ho Gym.

Just having Nana and her junkie-looking pale assistants in front of the gym was generating some good attention. When the tourists saw our fake stars, they all started pointing and taking pictures. When we began to seriously shoot, a freakishly early Santa Ana wind arrived and made our actors begin to look more like refugees in a scene from *Desert Storm,* the film. First, Angelina's wig blew off. Then Matt's aviator glasses flew off his face and his slicked down boy-next-door hair stuck straight up like a cock's comb, making him look more like a punk singer than a leading man, and we had to cancel the shoot. It was a disaster. I suppose one of us benefited from the shoot: I saw Halo jump in Nana's red Lamborghini and take off, into the hot dusty wind, just in time for me to catch a glimpse of her personalized license plate—SNATCH!

To Franco With Love

• • • • • • • • • •

MAXI'S NEXT BIG IDEA was to have "guest trainers" that we could advertise, not just on our website but in other gyms. So Maxi interviewed trainers living in New York City to give the promotion an exotic flair, and found a guy that he simply referred to as "Franco the Yankee." When he first arrived to the gym, we were all slightly shocked by his appearance. He was tallish, Hispanic, with a wide tribal tattoo around his bicep. He had thick rings of black hair, but the most surprising thing about Franco was that by California standards—as a trainer—he had big arms, but was a tad chunky in the midsection.

When we teased Maxi about it, he just shrugged. "So what! I'm chubby and I am strong like bull!" On his first day, Franco walked down to Big Daddy's Pizza on the corner and brought back three huge slices of greasy pizza. And *actually* stood at the front desk and ate it on my counter.

Franco loved to talk, and he was entertaining. He gave me his entire life story within the first hour. He was first-generation Dominican, originally from Santo Domingo. He was proud to remind me that Santo Domingo was where Columbus departed from the New World to return to Spain on his first voyage to the Americas, and that it was the true resting place of the explorer's bones.

When Franco, his mom, and little brother, which he referred to as the "Nina," the "Pinta, and the "Santa Maria," arrived to the

United States, they moved to Flatbush, Brooklyn. Even though Vanessa grew up in Brooklyn, they might as well have been born on different planets.

Franco told me, "Yeah, we grew up with Jewish landlords that always complained about the grease smell in our apartment. Mom fried everything and she taught me to fry everything. I was two hundred pounds by the time I was twelve years old. Mom was always gone and working, so I watched my baby brother. The lucky thing for me was that a neighbor, who was my football coach, took an interest in me and agreed to train me on the weekends. Man, I had to get up at five-thirty a.m. on Saturdays, but it paid off. I was an All-City, All-State tight end and got a full scholarship to play ball at Morrisville State College."

I liked Franco. I liked his moxie. I did my best to sell him as a trainer to prospective members. It was tough because we didn't have any machines or traditional gym equipment and he was not used to the natural athletic classes we offered, but he quickly created his own class, inspired by Halo's boot-camp approach, that he called the "Brooklyn Crunch." It was a mixture of mat Pilates, strength training, and boot-camp basics. Over the next couple of weeks, he actually built up the class, mostly from his buddies at Big Daddy's Pizza. As it happens, the chunkier clients felt more comfortable with a chunkier trainer! Bingo.

In between classes, Franco would hold court at the front desk and I loved it because he and the other trainers would share their personal philosophy about training. And that would lead to my favorite entertainment: war stories about crazy clients.

Franco launched into a story about his gym in Manhattan. "Man, it's tough training in Manhattan. I worked in a 'No Judgment Gym' in Chelsea that attracted the craziest people in Manhattan. I had to get up at two-thirty a.m. to eat breakfast. Then I run to catch the train and have seven stops and got to the gym at four thirty for my first client, Peter Paxton, at five a.m.

"This dude was a trip. He was twenty-three years old, six-three, and one hundred and twenty pounds. He was originally from the Midwest, graduated from college, and now lived with his brother, across the street from the gym and *insisted* on meeting at five a.m. He had quit his real estate job to go into 'film' and had to be on set really early. His fitness goal was to gain fifteen pounds of muscle and get six-pack abs because he had a new boyfriend that worked in fashion and always mentioned his stomach.

"He was adamant that *he did not want to sweat*. The first day, I strapped the ankle bands on him to do some leg strengthening on a machine and before I could get it secure on his ankle, he snapped at me, 'Wait, I'm not doing this. I am not a dog, Franco. You can't just tie me up!'

"When he didn't do a routine well, he would flick his hair and say, 'I am *just not* a morning person!' Every time, it got more difficult not to strangle the guy. The end came when he stormed in one morning late for our appointment. He walked over to me at the front desk, and almost in tears, shouted, 'Franky, I have *zits*... and I think it is from— you!' Man, I just couldn't do it anymore..."

Rex loved to talk to Franco; he referred to Franco as a "plantain," a good old-fashioned brown brother from the 'hood that understood what was what in life. As Rex told Maxi: "He is *nasty* and I don't really trust a man that ain't *nasty!*"

Rex told us about his crazy clients when he worked in West Hollywood. "Children, you don't know crazy until you work in Hollywood! My favorite was Richard the Treadmill Guy. This crazy man had a disco in his own mind, and on that treadmill. He would dance and then slide right off the back of the machine, dance some more, get back on, and slide right back off and start Vogueing, posing, and throwing his arms every which way. He made Madonna look like a spastic schoolgirl! He told me, 'First, I put on my party music to get happy. Then, I get sassy, and finally I finish off fierce, by Vogueing.' Don't you know we had our own

Ghetto Fab Ball every time that fool came to the gym! Come to think of it, I need to add a Voodoo Vogue Class to my schedule!"

"Well, that is just fine. I am going to add a Friday night Strip Tease Class!" Vanessa said. Then she talked about a fight she had with Madonna back in New York, and said she still has the earring that she pulled out of Madonna's ear. Then came more stories about her New York clients.

"OMG, I had a transsexual in my class that insisted on wearing red stilettos. You should've seen her downward dogs in those things! And later, in the locker room, forget about it! This woman cleared it out. She was all hairy body and *new* big boobs.

"Baby that shit would scare me too, it's like having a Sasquatch in the shower with you…"

"No, Rex, it's like having a Sas-crotch in the shower!"

"Oh my God, you two are sick!" I said, putting my hands over my face.

"Well, baby, one day I came to work and they had found a dead man in the steam sauna."

Halo jumped in. "At my last gym in San Diego, on base, I had to close up the place. We always yelled 'fifteen minutes' into the women's locker room to give them heads up and then we yelled 'We are closed,' wait five minutes, and then go in and clean up towels and make sure everything was locked down. One night, I did the usual routine and walked into the ladies' locker room and one of the members was laying with her eyes shut, totally oblivious to me, with her legs spread and hooked over the side, pushed up against the hot-tub jets, having a good old time!"

"Is that how they jet-ski in San Diego?" Rex asked laughing uncontrollably.

"It is amazing to me how many people come to the gym and don't do shit," Franco said. "Back home we had lots of men, famous men, 'respectable men,' and powerful married men that would come in, go straight to the men's locker room, get naked and go sit in the steam room, shower, and then leave." He looked at Rex, as if expecting him to supply an answer.

"Well, baby, but that is something *different* and too long a story to talk about here..." Rex said, arching his eyebrows.

"Guys, *right now* I have an older female client, she is a psychologist," Halo said. "Always uses medical terms to explain why she can't do something, 'I can't do this today because my C-4 is out' or 'my coccyx is bothering me.' Something is *always* 'out' and she is going to the physical therapist, or the chiropractor, or this or that specialist. After several sessions, I decided to bring it to her attention. It seemed to be a really unhealthy pattern. I very politely asked her about it and she burst out crying. I was freaking out, oh my God, what had I done? Then she tells me she thinks that it is because she was sexually abused when she was three years old by her father." Halo was obviously slightly unnerved by it.

Something about his story wasn't funny. It hit me so hard that I unexpectedly began to feel a panic attack and quickly excused myself to the women's restroom. I didn't bring my backpack and had no candy corns, so I just shoved my finger down my throat until I threw up. I was choking and crying uncontrollably, and then the restroom door opened.

A second later, the stall door opened and was hitting my legs. I looked up, horrified that I had been discovered. Plato picked me up and hugged me like a child. He gently touched my head and said, "Now, now sweet friend, it's all going to be OK. We will talk about this later and work it out—I promise."

Plato was the first person to find out about my purging problem and somehow I was OK with that, it felt right, as if I knew subconsciously that he could be the help I needed. I tried to stop crying and thanked him and agreed to go to his apartment later and talk. I washed my face with cold water for like five minutes until I could regain my composure.

Back to the front desk, only Franco remained. Rex and Halo had gone to lunch and Vanessa went to Juicy for lemongrass-ginger tea. Franco was doing his best to make me cheer up and he knew that Halo's story really upset me, but he didn't know why. He was nice enough to not ask. After a few minutes, we were back on crazy clients, gym gossip, and laughing together.

Apti walked in and bluntly asked if his next client, Justin, was in the gym. He didn't give me his usual big loving smile. He seemed distracted and put out about something. He just said, "Tell Justin I am waiting for him at the Skate Park!"

When he left, Franco said, "Somebody is grumpy!"

"Oh, he probably injured himself again and isn't letting on."

"No, I think it is something else. If I had to guess, he doesn't like me standing here laughing with you."

"What, are you crazy in the head?"

Vanessa walked by and said, "Yeah, well you know what they say, crazy in the head, crazy in bed!"

It caused me to blush. Franco ignored Vanessa. "I'm serious, kid. That guy loves you."

"Well, he sure has a unique way of demonstrating it!"

"It's a cultural thing. It is the same in the Dominican Republic. If a guy likes a girl, he expects her to act a certain way and he doesn't like it when another guy hangs out laughing with his girl. Back home, a guy can get killed doing that!"

"First, I am not '*his* girl.' So, what, if you like someone in Chechnya, you give them the stink-eye and ignore them?"

"No, but you sure as hell don't flaunt it in public if you are interested in her. Well, if you're so sure that Apti doesn't want to go out with you… I would like to ask you out." Franco said, jokingly.

Apti walked in and heard the last part of the sentence, "I would like to ask you out." He snapped an icy glare at Franco, turned slowly to me and said, "So, still no Justin?"

"No, and he's usually so punctual. Do you want me to call him?"

"No, he is already over thirty minutes late. His mother respects our sessions and me about as much as she does a valet parking her car at a restaurant. Would you like to go have lunch with me?"

"Go on, Barbella, I am happy to watch the front. Besides, it gives me an opportunity to work on promoting my class!" Franco said encouragingly, trying to let Apti know that he had no intention of getting between us.

I was freaking out inside, *Apti Murid was asking me out to lunch?* I nonchalantly said, "Cool," and went to get my backpack. But just as I was walking toward the front door, my dad walked in. Of all the times for him to decide to visit me, he comes now—really? I found it hard to say anything other than, "Dad!"

He grabbed me. "How is my little princess *the trainer* doing? I have really missed you. I thought I would come by and see if you wanted to grab a bite to eat for lunch?" I turned to introduce Apti and he was gone. Without any opportunity to look, or wait for him, Dad rushed me out of the gym and into his illegally parked Hummer right in front of the gym. "Dad, you know you can't park here, right?" I asked in a pseudo-bitchy way. He just grinned. "So sue me. I am friends with, and have trained, every judge in Los Angeles!"

Dad insisted that we first go and see my new apartment. Once inside, he snooped around, trying to act like he was just checking the place out. He looked in my fridge, to make sure I was eating healthy foods, and then my garbage can, I suppose for beer bottles. While he was still in the kitchen, someone knocked on my front door. My heart leapt, from the surprise and the certainty that it was Apti. I was excited to have the chance to introduce him to my dad. When I quickly opened the door, I was even more surprised.

"Mom! I didn't expect to see you today…"

"I know, honey, I just was in the neighborhood and thought I would drop by and see if you wanted to grab a quick bite to eat," she said sweetly, as she just pushed past me, and walked into the apartment.

"Well actually, Dad is here and he was just about to take me to lunch. Do you want to join us?" I tried to say in an inviting manner, secretly praying she would say no and leave before he came into the room.

"Hello, Laurie, it's been awhile. You sure haven't changed." Dad walked into the living room from the kitchen.

"It has been Renzo, it certainly has," Mom said, clearly trying to be nice.

"Would you like to join us? We are going over to the Firehouse to talk about Bar's new job…"

"Thank you, I needed to talk to her about some other things, just the two of us, girl talk, thanks anyway."

I could tell that Mom came to tell me something serious, but was about to claw her way out of the apartment, she was so uncomfortable. I hadn't been in the same room with them since I was a baby. They both looked really sad.

"Mom, thanks for coming by. I will call you later."

"OK honey. Bye, Renzo," Mom said, passively.

"Bye," Dad said, with a lingering tone of melancholy.

After he poked around my apartment a bit more, and was satisfied that I wasn't having teenage orgies and that Mom was long gone, we hopped back into his car and headed to The Firehouse.

Finally, I couldn't take it anymore and blurted out, "So Dad, when are you and Mom going to get over this stuff. For Christ's sake, it's been almost eighteen years!"

"Bar, I am sorry. What can I do? I'm nice and I try. What do you want me to do—beg her to forgive me for some stupid thing I did eighteen years ago?"

I couldn't help myself and decided not to hold back any more. "Well, Dad, actually, I do expect you to beg her for her forgiveness. You were a self-centered pig. She was pregnant and in love with you and you banged a South African slut in the ally at Gold's, left her to raise me alone, and didn't help out financially. You're obsessed with sex and youth, and so I can sort of see why she assumed the worst when... well, you know. Yes, I think you should be the one to step up and make the amends."

Dad didn't say a word, but I could tell he was upset. I just stared out the window in silence.

He drove up Dudley Court toward Main Street. As we went up the alley, I could see the Frank Gehry binocular building, which made me feel so sad that Apti and I didn't get the chance to have lunch, that I couldn't introduce my dad, and that my parents seemed so uncomfortable to be in the same room together. *Was it always going to be like that? What if I get married some day and have a family?* I comforted myself by thinking something utterly obscure: *if it is meant to be, it will be!*

When we got to Main and Sunset, I saw Apti skating toward the Giggle building and had the distinct feeling he was up to no good.

At the Firehouse, Dad and I ordered our usual and he asked me the same old questions. How was getting certified going? Did I have a boyfriend? Nothing I wanted to chat about. So he talked about himself: his girlfriend and his television show. About the old gang, and how Arnold was finally starting to show his age. About the famous clients he still trained.

My ears perked up. "So, Dad, do you think you might be interested in being a guest trainer at Maxi's? And could you get any of your famous clients to come to the gym?"

He wasn't really keen on the idea because Maxi's gym was a "natural" gym, and he was a steroid-chomping, iron-pumping, old school plate-slapping Gym Rat.

"Jeez, honey, they don't even have a freakin' barbell rack," Dad said. "Between you and me, kid, that gym is never going to make money. It is tough to make money with a gym. You have to have a lot of new members joining every month, sell a ton of add-ons, merchandise, supplements, or charge a butt load of money for memberships. Either way, darling, Maxi's gym doesn't have any of that going for it. He will have to invest in equipment, and that is *extremely expensive*. He'll probably have to create an upstairs, locker rooms, steam sauna and hot tubs, towels and laundry service, and parking. He needs to find at least four hundred thousand dollars to invest in the place.

"Besides, who would have the *cojones* to compete directly against Gold's in Venice Beach? Gold's is known around the world as *the home of bodybuilding*, Gold's and Muscle Beach. Do you really think Ho Gym can compete with that?"

I didn't say much. The whole thing made me sick and sad for Maxi, myself, the gang, and definitely made me want to eat some candy corns. And that made me even sadder.

• • •

When I got back to the gym, I really had to snap out of my daddy coma. Our conversation at lunch really depressed me. He made it seem like all this was hopeless. I had to remind myself that in a short time, with virtually nothing, the gym had come so far. It was struggling financially, but I'm not sure anyone who walked through the front door would know. We gave great classes and everyone had such a good attitude. Everyone truly cared. In just over three months, I felt closer and had more love for the gang than I did for anyone after three years at Miss Palmer's School. I felt like I could be one-hundred-percent myself, *and that* made me feel rich.

Where would I go if this didn't work out? This uncertainty seemed to light a fire under me to complete my training certification. After work, I would go straight home and study until midnight and maybe I would be ready for the final exam next week and could finally get some personal clients. *Somehow, it would all work out. Things always did.*

Just before we closed, Plato came up front and started sweeping the floors. I knew that he was waiting to talk to me about why I was crying earlier when he found me in the women's restroom. I didn't really want to talk to him. I was still tired from Dad's little discussion, but he kept glancing over, and giving me big loving eyes. He made his way to the front desk. "Well, darling, I won't disturb you for long, just a brief word. A very wise person once told me, and 'This too shall pass!'"

"I know, Plato. I don't know what got me into today."

"Hum, if you are *quiet enough,* and listen *deeply* to your feelings, I bet you'll know why you are doing this to yourself. Once, I cultivated some pretty crappy ideas about myself that were very critical and hard. I was always secretly in a state of fear, with feelings of insecurity lurking quietly. Never felt like I was *enough.* Always had to accomplish the next *big thing* that would prove to everyone that I was. As it happens, it was just a stupid idea that I picked up as a kid, that no longer served me, but I didn't know how to let it go. In other words, I held *myself* a prisoner for no good reason. Wow, how fucking sad is that?

"All I really want to say, lovely girl, is that you are not a prisoner. You can let it go and you will, when you are ready. You are lovely and you're more than 'enough.' In fact, you are radiantly beautiful, the embodiment of abundance in every way, and I am so very pleased to know you."

I didn't know what to say, so I held my hands in prayer position and said, "Namaste." He returned the prayer with his lovely shining eyes.

For some reason, I really wanted to reconnect with Mom. It had been an emotionally intense day. I called her, but she didn't answer. I decided to go home and study for my Trainer certification.

• • •

Once at home, I really didn't feel like cooking dinner, so I ate almonds, fresh avocado, and some sliced turkey. I was determined to work on my study materials for my certification. After literally growing up in a gym, and now working in one, I was having a really hard time finding the material stimulating. It was material like:

As a Personal Fitness Trainer, you should be able to deliver the following:

- *Knowledge of human anatomy, concepts of functional exercise, basic nutrition, and basic exercise science.*

- *An ability to design individual and group exercise programs tailored to the needs and goals of specific clients.*

- *An ability to motivate others to improve their overall fitness and health.*

I was so bored that I slapped my face to stay awake, rubbed ice cubes over my forehead, danced a disco song or two, did sets of crunches, got up for spiced almonds and walnuts, and finally handfuls of salty seaweed chips. If my mouth was chewing, then I couldn't fall asleep. Or so I thought, until I was startled awake by a tapping sound on my window. Followed by another tap. That one really woke me up, and scared the hell out of me. Then, a third tap and I realized that someone was throwing small pebbles at my window.

I went to the window and looked out and didn't see anyone, until I saw a guy walking on his hands down the alley in the moonlight, and knew it had to be Apti.

"What in the hell are you doing in my alley at this time of night?" I said, acting as if I was incensed.

Apti said in an exaggerated Russian accent, "First, this is not your alley. I have lived here much longer than you. Secondly, sorry I missed lunch today."

He apologized for coming at such a late hour, but he noticed the lights on and wanted to explain his disappearance earlier today. I invited him in for midnight tea.

The moment he walked in, I felt warm, alive and nervous, like I did that day on the bridge when he kissed me. He complimented the apartment and seemed to really appreciate Sophie's amazing paintings. When we settled into drinking our tea, I sat on the small couch and he sat on the floor with his back against it. He told me he lived down the street. That was why, the first day I saw him running from the Giggle security cops, he ran over the rooftops, to get home.

I asked him what the symbol on his skateboard meant, the heart with the wings. And what was the Russian expression he screamed from the rooftop? The symbol, he said, represented the Sufi order of Islam. I didn't have a clue what he was referring to, although I did remember reading something about a Persian poet named Rumi at Miss Palmer's and I think he was somehow associated with the Sufi. He told me the Russian expression "Бог велик," that sounded like *Bor-he-lick*, meant, "God is great."

I wanted to ask him so many questions about his childhood, his beliefs, about his culture, about coming to America, but I didn't want to freak him out. It was obvious that he wasn't accustomed to sharing personal information.

As if he read my heart and mind, he started talking. "I feel the need to explain some things. My life is very complicated. Let me say that first, and foremost I really like you, Barbella, and I truly care about you. I think you are beautiful."

"You have a strange way of showing it!" I responded, slightly uncomfortable.

"I know it must appear that way to you. I need to explain some things for you to understand. Back home, 'dating' is not part of our social life for young people. In Venice, my father has been very strict with me and discouraged me from getting involved with an

American girl. He always says, 'Love is not some fast-food drive-through. He wants me to marry a Chechen girl.'"

"Are you saying you can't see me because I'm an American?"

"No. I am saying that it is complicated."

"I would really like you to explain what you mean by *complicated*, please."

"OK, first, you know that I am Chechen. I live here, but my heart is in Chechnya. I believe that heart comes from God. As a Sufi, I walk a very simple path. We call it *tawhid*. Think of God, the beloved, as the deepest spiritual root from which, as humans, we have been cut off and we long and desire to be restored, reconnected. Rumi believed passionately that music, poetry, and dance could be a path to reach God. *My path* is skating and parkour. When I am running and using my body with all my strength, I feel connected to God, to my family and to my culture."

Apti put his head into his hands and stopped talking.

"My lovely mother, Sandrine Degenes, and my baby sister, Madeleine, were at a hospital during the second Russian invasion. My mother was a volunteer nurse and trying to care for the wounded Chechen freedom fighters. The schools were closed, so everyone brought their children to work. Russian soldiers wearing black masks marched into the hospital and dragged everyone out, marched them to an open grave, put the staff and their children in a line, and executed them, one by one.

"By the time me and my father and the other men arrived, I just recognized my mother by her dress. It had flowers from Provence. It was her favorite. She told me it made her happy, so she could help make other people happy. My sister's Russian baby doll was still attached to her bloody hand."

I gently stroked his neck and back and softly said, "It's OK." He turned to me with pain-filled tears in his eyes. "I was supposed to watch my baby sister, Madeleine, that day and my father insisted that I help my grandmother instead.

"My father tells me, 'Whatever happens in your life, no matter how troubling things might seem, do not despair. Even when all doors remain closed, God will open up a new path only for you. Be thankful!' A Sufi is supposed to be thankful not only for what he has been given but also for all that he has been denied, but I am just *so fucking angry.*'"

"Your dad sounds amazing and wise. I would love to meet him some day."

"Well, that is another complexity, and that is why I disappeared today when your father came to the gym. My father had to return to Chechnya to care for my grandmother, who is not doing well. We only have one other living relative to care for her, but she is too old and sick. I don't know when he can return to the United States and he told me the Russians are giving him a hard time because he left Chechnya as a doctor, when his 'country' needed him. I am really worried about him. It is so difficult for me to explain the situation. I didn't want your father to think that his daughter is dating a crazy terrorist!"

"Oh, are we *dating*? You have a very strange way of showing it! You practically ignore me every day."

"Well, you are too busy flirting with Franco to notice much else!"

"Franco? Are you crazy? I don't flirt with Franco. He is just nice to me, helps me with my trainer certification, and gives me tips on training clients. How is that flirting? You and I have never even been out together—not once!"

"What did you call the night on the bridge—bowling?"

"That was a thank-you kiss for rescuing my backpack."

"So you kiss anyone that does something nice for you?"

"What a minute, buddy, you are crossing the line." I was getting agitated. *Just because I kissed a guy once doesn't give him authority over me*, I don't care what culture or country he is from.

"I am sorry. You're right. In Chechnya, if we kiss someone, it means that we are completely dedicated to that person. It means we *truly* care, and it means that we want you to become a *true* friend. Our friendships last a lifetime. Here, people become your 'friend' in ten minutes and say 'I love you,' and when you need them, they are not available.

"My kiss was not *just* a kiss. It was to show you that I care about you. I'm sorry that I didn't take the time to share this with you before tonight. I've been in a great deal of conflict about my father, my Giggle project, and I didn't want to distract you from studying for your training certification. And. I've been trying to build up my training business, and, how do you say, 'Stay my head on the water' financially."

"No, the expression is, keep my head *above* water," I said, with some much needed laughter. When the laughter subsided, I said: "What is your Giggle project? What is your problem with Giggle anyway?"

"I don't have a problem with Giggle. I think the search engine is fantastic—too fantastic—for Putin to use as a resource to exploit innocent people in Chechnya, the Ukraine, and Russia. The real question for me is why one of the Giggle founders, Serge Brantov, would even allow Giggle into Russia after what his poor father and family endured."

"What?" I was completely ignorant to what he was discussing.

"Serge's family lived in Moscow and as a young man his father wanted to be an astronomer. He gave up his dream because, as a Jew, he already knew that the Communist Party wouldn't permit a Jew entry into the best universities, and particularly excluded them from prominent posts in physics. So, the family left Russia and came to America when Serge was six years old. His father wanted his son to have the freedom that he now enjoys so remarkably. Which begs the question, why does Giggle insist on doing business in Russia?

"Recently Putin changed the media laws. So now, a blogger with any kind of following has to register with the government. Stores must provide customer data to the government. Now the Kremlin can demand for content to be removed from the Internet if they deem it as an 'unsanctioned protest and unrest.' But then world advocates for Giggle in Russia say, 'Yes, but Giggle represents freedom of speech and it allows me to see important cultural sites like the Lavra Monastery in Moscow. Now is that freedom?' Freedom of religion is no problem in Russia, just freedom of speech!

"So in my own small way, I protest by skating on Giggle property, in front of Serge's precious binocular windows, to remind him, and his associates that they have enjoyed true freedom and prosperity, and in my humble opinion, they should use it wisely!"

It was all so *heavy* and hard for me to fully understand. I was exhausted and my eyes were getting heavy. He had so much passion and I loved listening to him talk about his home. There was so much I wanted to talk to him about, but I looked at the clock and it was two a.m. "Oh my God, it is so late and I have to open the gym tomorrow morning."

Apti got off the floor and stood in front of me. He extended his hand and helped pull me up. He gently wrapped his arms around me and pushed my head against his chest and I began to feel as if I could fly in his arms and plunge deep into the Tasman Sea and we could swim together in the warmth of the sun.

He soon left and I went straight to bed without any desire for candy corns. Just good, deep sleep, and another lingering hug from Apti.

In The Light of Day

• • • • • • •

THREE WEEKS LATER, I woke up Saturday morning before my alarm clock and felt deeply rested and super excited about the day ahead. I hadn't felt that way since I was twelve years old on Christmas. I finished studying for my trainer certification, took the exam on-line, and totally *nailed it*. I was officially a Fitness Trainer!

Everything seemed as if I was moving toward a wonderful new life. Not to mention being able to resist shoveling gobs of candy corns in my mouth and then purging. That was huge! Well, I did have a slight slip, after Maxi had another nervous breakdown about the gym and how we'd have to close if I didn't sell more memberships than I did last month.

"Try harder, Barbarella," Maxi would say. "Put more sexy Boom Boom in your sales pitch! Do you want to work as a checkout girl at the grocery store?"

But, if I am being honest, that didn't bother me because I was filled with the spirit of Apti. My body remembered what he felt like when he held me and kissed me, remembered his scent, and remembered the cute way he looked at me when he was feeling something, but didn't want to say it out loud. Wow, is this what they mean when they say they're falling in love with someone?

I still didn't have the courage to make coffee with Sandrine's fancy French machine, so I skated over to Groundwork Coffee Company and chatted with my barista buddy Gia. I asked her if I could leave some of my promo cards on the counter to advertise as a trainer. Apti designed some cool, sexy postcards for me. Nana's photography was amazing. She actually had me looking *Ho-sizzle* with all that red paint splattered on my body. Apti also designed a one-page website with a cool video of me talking about my training philosophy, working out, and some free-running routines.

I had already gotten several calls, mostly from pervy high-school boys asking if I would train their little friend "Richard" and whip him into shape and help him to get bigger and really hard? Then they screamed with laughter and hung up.

I hadn't introduced Apti to Dad yet, but Mom has had us over for dinner about four times and thinks he is adorable and, I think, likes him as much as I do. Apti is really sweet to her, and Tonya. He even helped Tonya with some posing moves, and gave her some great balance exercises to get her ready for her upcoming bodybuilding competition.

Tonya keeps insisting that I should enter the competition in the Natural category. Mom was touchy on the subject and launched into her diatribe: "People need to respect what God gave them and know their limitations. If you're going to call yourself a 'bodybuilder,' then train like one by educating yourself. Or you're just another idiot at the gym working out incorrectly, waiting for the next injury." Then she shared horror stories about professional trainers.

Apti shared amusing accounts of the guys at his American high school and the stupid things they did in the gym. There was one standard scrawny kid who put too much weight on the bench press bar, with no spotter. Of course, he pressed it up and it came straight down onto his neck, pinning him down, and the little tough guy started screaming like a girl for help.

Apti's favorite was a guy who stood in front of the mirror flexing and doing Kung Fu moves, very self-enthralled, and then pressing dead weights over his head. He would jerk them up, his back arched like a stray cat, breathing like a bull in the ring, spit flying from his mouth. He would do this eight times, and then drop the bar from the height of his chest—a crashing, thunderous thud to the mat. Everyone in the gym would jump up nervously, worried that an earthquake was hitting the gym.

I told them about all the folks at our gym that come in before their group class, to "warm up" with their own moves. A Giggle guy named Kenneth liked to lay on his back with his legs over his head doing the bicycle, then donkey kicks, then a free-form movement that looked like some kind of crazy octopus modern dancer. Or Charlie, who liked to lay over the bouncy ball and hunch it, instead of doing stomach crunches on it, throwing his arms around spastically.

Also amusing are the yoga folks who try to force the *asana*, or pose, to look more advanced. They are the ones that are constantly making massage appointments at YO due to a pulled this or an achy that. Apti smiled. "You know that in India, yoga was to prepare the practitioner for meditation, not to make their bum look cute in tight pants!"

Well, this is my new life: talking twenty-four hours, seven days a week about fitness, training, nutrition, and health. It had always been there, but this was *my life* now, my career, and it felt great. I certainly knew how to train my own body, but I wasn't sure about someone else's. Also, the people around me in the past were already years into their training. What would I do to inspire the chubby person, or someone that had never exercised in their life?

When I got to the gym, Plato was in the yoga studio meditating. Maxi was back in his office cursing in Korean and I could hear his conversation peppered with words in English like, "interest rate, "payoff amount," and finally, "Are you *fucking* kidding me?" I was determined to stay positive. We hadn't opened and already it was promising to be a challenging day filled with more schemes, plans, and big ideas from Maxi. When he finally ended his call, he came storming up to the front desk. "OK, Barbie, the shit has hit the air conditioning!"

"No, Maxi, 'the shit has hit the fan'!"

"OK, OK hit the fan! Either way, we are in trouble! The bank said it would close down the gym if I don't come up with forty thousand dollars by the end of the month. That gives me four weeks to make that money. That means we have to sign up eight hundred new members in one month or we are exercising on the beach! Wait, that gives me a great idea!"

Just as Maxi was explaining his idea for volleyball on the beach, a guy walked in. I knew immediately that he was a high tech-guy, but not at Giggle. We had several of those guys. They all had a special air-conditioned quality that suggested, *We are young and rich*, like they hadn't rolled in the dirt in their lifetime. This guy was different. He looked slightly less "happy." He had blond hair and expensive dark sunglasses, a nice shirt with khaki shorts and expensive running shoes with no socks. I guessed he was around fifty. He drove a black BMW four-wheel drive that he parked illegally by the door, and the first thing he said was, "Is it OK if I park there for a minute?"

There was something immediately appealing about him. He wasn't arrogant like the yoga bitches. He seemed humble but super capable. "No, you're good," I said, trying to sound positive in the face of the fact that we don't open for another thirty minutes and that Maxi had just gone into an apoplectic fit.

Then, the miracle occurred. The guy politely explained that he was staying in Venice for a six-month contract with a nearby high-tech firm and felt he needed to get in better shape. He saw my postcard at Groundwork Coffee Company this morning, and Gia, the barista, said he should hire me as his personal trainer. Maxi swooped in and insisted that he join the gym — today! And added that the guy's training sessions would be thirty percent cheaper per hour. And that over the six months, he'd see a significantly offset membership cost. And as an added benefit, he could take advantage of other great offers at the gym at a lower rate.

Of course, *we don't have* any other "great offers," but it didn't seem to matter. The guy agreed and pulled out his credit card, ready to join Maxi Ho Gym on the spot. We quickly did the paperwork and he wanted to start right away. The best part was that he wanted to train with me three times per week. His name was Keegan Macleod and he was my new favorite person on earth. Well, second most favorite person.

We set up our first training session for later in the day, at three p.m. and I was so excited I could hardly concentrate on my opening duties. I just wanted to dance and jump up and down. Maxi was further freaked out by the reality that I wouldn't be at the front desk in the afternoon. I explained that Vanessa and Franco already said they would watch the front, for free, while I trained.

"What? Nobody work for free in this world. What are they up to?" Maxi snipped.

"Don't worry, Maxi, it will all work out."

"Easy for you to say, little Barbie. You don't have the bank trying to slit your juggling vein!"

Maxi was becoming unbearable. I screamed, "It's a jugular vein, Maxi—and no one is trying to cut yours!"

Fear was bringing out the worst in Maxi and making everyone feel bad. We'd all worked so hard to make this gym a reality and to bring something special to Venice, but the financial stress was starting to affect everyone. The only thing I knew how to do was to be the best damn trainer I knew how to be and try and bring a positive attitude to work. I decided to organize a trainers' night out to boost everyone's morale. I knew that Rex would be the perfect person to help me put together something really fun.

By lunchtime, I needed to get out of the gym, so I skated home to have a chicken and kale salad. I couldn't find Apti. I didn't have much time and I needed to think about my session with Keegan. I skated quickly up Pacific Avenue. At Sunset, I saw my dad's car turning in the other direction. He was leaving Gold's. I realized that he and I hadn't trained once together since I came back from school. Every Tuesday felt a little sad with all the great memories of us in the gym together. All the laughter and jokes we shared. I loved all the muscle boys flirting with me playfully, and him busting their chops to protect me. He'd say, "Bar, you gotta start wearing baggy clothes to the gym." And I would drive him nuts by responding, "Baggy is haggy—*no way*—Daddy!"

I started feeling down and wanted to pop a candy corn. I stopped myself and realized, *Wow, I still have some unresolved anger and resentment about his three-year absence in my life, but I don't have to resolve this today.* I was determined not to let this detour my most excellent mood. Maybe Dad was wrong about the Ho gym. Maybe we would make it. After all, wasn't that what he was up against every time he trained for a competition—the *uncertainty*—and the sheer determination to win at all cost?

When I got to Dudley Court, I heard loud whistles blowing, and two men screaming, "Stop and put your arms up—now!" I looked up the alley to see the Gehry Binoculars—and Apti flying down the hill on his skateboard. He saw me and flashed a big smile. As he flew down the hill a Venice Beach police car screeched to a halt beside me, sirens blasting, to block the alley. Apti had a familiar look in his eye, the look I'd seen so many times just before he did something amazing and crazy. When he got to the parked cop car, he jumped on top of the hood and ran across, then jumped back onto his board on the other side.

But two more cop cars had arrived, and the officers jumped out and drew their guns, screaming, "On the fucking ground, kid, or this will be your last day in Venice."

Apti stopped and threw his hands above his head, faced the sky, and screamed, "Бог велик" (God is great) and lay down.

I ran over to the cops. They turned and pointed their guns directly in my face and screamed, "Freeze." One of the officers came over and made me open my backpack. I tried to explain that I was a friend of Apti's and he barked, "This is none of your concern and you need to move on, or I will arrest you as an accomplice!"

"An accomplice to what?" I asked.

"Breaking and entering on private property."

"Where are you taking him?" I asked as the cop returned to Apti.

"None of your business."

"Yes it is. I am his girlfriend and his father is in Europe."

He ignored me, and focused on getting Apti handcuffed and in the car. I was trying not to cry, but I was so mad I couldn't help it. Apti saw me, and I heard him cursing loudly in Chechen as the cops sped away.

At home, I felt too upset to eat. *What was I going to do to help Apti? I couldn't tell my dad—he hadn't even meet Apti. My mom would be too upset and she was broke. Maybe Maxi had an attorney that could help?* By the time I calmed down, I had to get back to the gym. I decided to stop thinking about Apti until after my first session with Keegan. It would all work out somehow. I would find a way.

I tried to concentrate on how I would train Keegan. I would start him with thirty minutes of cardio—power walking—at first, and then bring him back for some core and upper-body strength training and conclude with some nice, slow stretching.

When I got back to the gym, Vanessa momentarily distracted me at the front desk with a story about one of our members named Hellena. She was a tall, lovely Englishwoman with long white hair who loved to engage with everyone. Hellena's usual introduction was to notice something about someone—their bag, or a garment—and ask something like, "Oh, is that top from the new Calvin Klein yoga line? Well, it certainly is attention-getting… seems just perfect for the downward dog." She would flash an ironic glance toward a tall, good-looking male member, followed by an infectiously naughty smile. Vanessa said that today, Hellena was chatting with a distraught member who had lost her cat and found it dead in the canal. Hellena listened sympathetically, but later, before leaving gym, she yelled across the room to the woman, "Sorry about your pussy, Love!"

"*Now what happened* to Miss Thang's pussy?" Rex inquired.

Everyone burst out laughing. I couldn't help myself: "It seems she found it floating in the canal!"

"Now, little Miss Jackie O, you are not right in the head!"

"Oh, finally a subject you know something about, Rex—head!" Vanessa lobbed.

"As a matter of fact, I was just at a wine tasting with some of my lady clients from class and Miss Urma poured me a glass of Reserve Monducci… and I said, 'Ummmmm, fruity, Mr. Monducci, but a tad bit flaccid!' And those white girls commenced to giggle, and I damn near thought they would *pinot noir* on themselves."

At that precise moment, Keegan walked in, carrying a Tupperware container. He looked at Rex. "Well, then is it safe to assume there is not a 'tinkle of hope' that they *will ever* drink Monducci again? Get it, pinot on themselves, *tinkle*…"

"Oh Lord, this gym is in *pun*-demonium!" Rex fired back.

Everyone was introduced to Keegan, and then he opened his plastic container and offered everyone a delicious-looking chocolate brownie, informing us that he got the recipe from Thomas Keller at The French Laundry, but had improved it slightly.

Rex ate one. "Who brings brownies to a gym before they work out? You are just a devil!"

"So I guess you like the 'work of the devil'?"

Rex raised his arm in the air. "Oh Lord, more than your little pitchfork could ever know!"

I stepped up. "OK, that's it. I've had enough man-gination for one day. Time to work out, Chef Punny Macleod!"

"Yes, ma'am, and please, call me Keegan!"

I quickly replied, "Well then, is it safe to assume that I am not the *Apple* of your eye since you will not allow me to call you Mr. *Mac*-cloud?"

Keegan turned his head. "Not terribly funny, technology humor, but lightning fast—nice!"

Four

The Guy In the White Hat

• • • • • • • • • • • • • •

IT WAS HARD to concentrate on my first session with Keegan. I was nervous, and worried about Apti. After some basic warm-up stretches, I took Keegan outside for a power walk. His skin was electric white and I was determined to get him a complimentary tan as part of the training. You just don't walk around Venice in the summer looking as white as the Poppin' Fresh guy! Within five minutes, he began to sound winded and perspire heavily. I said, "Good job, buddy — way to hustle — let's go!"

He gave me a sideways stare that implied, *Really? Do you have to be so patronizingly enthusiastic and obvious with your trainer jargon?* I decided to distract him with questions. "So, Keegan, tell me more about what you do for a living?"

Sadly, I can't recall much that he told me for the first twenty minutes, because he went way over my ability to understand his science/technology background, but I do remember that he attended M.I.T. to study physics, later something with laser technology and satellites, and something about military contracts with the DoD, then fiber-optic technology, and developing technology for Broadband Internet. He retired at thirty-nine to bake, write country-and-western songs, and children's poems. He plays the guitar, and loves Jimi Hendrix, especially the song "All Along the Watchtower." He talked about how he is lonely and wants to find someone to love *him*, not his nest egg. He was as brilliant and complicated as a good soufflé.

Then Keegan turned. "So, when you are not training at the Maxi Ho gym, what gives your life lift? Or, is it safe to say you operate on Maximus *Ho*-lium'? Not to be mistaken of course with the rare earth element Holmium, the chemical element with symbol Ho and atomic number sixty-seven."

"No, my balloons are filled with *heal*-ium these days." I told him about my time at Miss Palmer's School.

"Wow, I bet you read a lot of Shakespeare!" Keegan grabbed my hand robotically, and in an accent that sounded like Monty Python meets C-3PO, said:

> *"If I profane with my unworthiest hand*
> *this holy shrine, the gentle sin is this:*
> *My lips, two blushing robot pilgrims, ready-stand*
> *to smooth that rough touch with a tender kiss."*

Without hesitation, I swooned like a blushing Renaissance maiden and replied,

> *"Good pilgrim, you do wrong your robot hand too much,*
> *Which mannerly devotion shows in this?*
> *For robots have hands that Wookiee pilgrims' hands do touch,*
> *And palm to palm is holy galactic Palmer's kiss."*

Keegan laughed and sweetly said, "So basically it ain't gonna happen?"

"Yeah, pretty much what that means. My boyfriend Apti might not approve!"

Keegan gave me a cute sideways smile. I loved that he was bright and that his flirtations were harmless and fun. I felt I was appreciated, deserving or not, by someone that understood and searched for beauty. If Miss Palmer's School had contributed anything to my education, beyond my desire to learn, it was in teaching me how to look beyond the surface of any comment or situation in search of a deeper meaning or truth.

"Is he Chechen?" Keegan asked. "Does he work for Giggle?"

"No, just visits occasionally," I said. "Why do you ask?"

"I just know that they like to hire young talent from the North Caucasus, Eastern Europe and Russian republics. The CIA and NSA love that shit!"

"What does the CIA have to do with Giggle?" I asked, totally confused.

"The bigger question is, what does Apti have to do with Giggle?"

"Complicated!" I said, hoping to end the line of questioning.

I found myself getting emotional. I had done a good job of not thinking about Apti during my session, but now the floodgate was about to break. I kept telling myself, *Keep it together, girl... you can do it... be strong... don't mess this up!*

When we got back in the gym. I suggested that we do some core strength training. It would be hard for Keegan to quiz me with a burning core. I showed him how to do a "plank" by supporting himself on his elbows, with his back straight and his legs fully extended. But after thirty seconds, he gave me a strong sideways glance and calmly said, "Please answer my question. What does Apti have to do with Giggle?"

Keegan could see the tears welling up as I changed his exercise to have him lie on his back and do crunches. I said, "Apti has frustrations with Giggle, because one of the founders is from Russia, and Apti believes that Putin and his military have used the search engine to gather information and use it against the Chechen people. Most of Apti's family was killed by the Russians in the last war."

Keegan listened carefully as he mopped his sweat-soaked forehead with his t-shirt. I sat on his feet, as counterweight, and instructed him to do sixty more crunches. I told him about the arrest and how freaked out I was. He remained quiet, but his mind sounded like my computer at home when it was really processing information. He didn't really say much during the rest of the session.

I had Keegan do as many push-ups as he could, followed by some curls and some other arm exercises with weights. Halo brought in his personal set from home since the gym couldn't afford equipment. Keegan burned out pretty quickly, so we switched to stretching. I had been taking Vanessa's yoga class and integrated some Hatha poses to help him get use to breathing and stretching at the same time. At the end of the one-hour session, he was soaked in sweat but seemed content.

He asked where the showers were and I pointed to the beach. "We are one-hundred-percent natural, buddy!"

"Do you have time to step to my car for a minute? I have an idea."

Between training him and telling him about Apti, I forgot to ask him about what the CIA had to do with Giggle. I went out to his car, and he pulled out a laptop and booted it up, he said, "I have a software app that will show us where Apti is by his cell phone number. We need to know if the cops took him to Giggle, or the City of Los Angeles Police Department." I gave him the number and in moments Keegan identified the location as the City of Los Angeles Police Headquarters.

This got me really upset because I didn't know how serious the charge would be or who could get him out of jail. No one I knew had any money for bail. Keegan looked at me with a determined smile. "I'll take care of it!" and walked around and got in the driver's seat. I tried to ask what he meant, but he cut me off. "Don't worry, I got this. Thanks for the session. I feel like a boiled buffalo!"

"Oh, then is it safe to say, given your haste, that you will soon sprout 'buffalo wings?'"

He smiled. "Yes, and you can be sure they will be *spicy*, my dear!"

I wasn't sure what "I'll take care of it" meant. *Should I have a backup plan in case he can't help Apti? Should I get over my fear and call Dad?*

Back inside, Vanessa was standing beside a young woman at the front desk explaining our classes. I'd never seen her before, so I knew she wasn't a member. Surely, Maxi hadn't hired another trainer in the face of our near economic disaster. We could barely pay for the electric bill, so how would we pay a new employee? The girl introduced herself as Raquel. She was in her early twenties and had an air of strength and calm, but didn't seem to try to draw attention to herself. She had long brown silky hair, and was thin and not terribly tall. She had on a purple t-shirt and long, black, training pants and wore really cool orange-and-purple running shoes.

Rex walked up. "What's happening, Purple Haze!" She just smiled. "Oh Lord, not another shy one! Where are you from, baby girl?"

"I am from Texas, but I've been teaching sports fitness, as an intern, at the University of Alabama. I was helping train the girls' volleyball team."

"Lord, that must have been some sad and lonely times. All those li'l white Southern Christian girls playing volleyball, saying, 'Oh darn it, I can't believe I missed that shot!' Rex started jumping up and down in his version of a spastic white girl playing volleyball.

"Well, actually, they were *really* nasty!" Raquel said.

"Oh, Baby Jesus—*nasty*—are you sure that is what you mean to say? Nasty how?"

"Do you know what 'clam slamming' is?"

"Yeah, we used to do that on the Jersey Shore. Bang the hell out of the clams with a hammer when they didn't open up," Vanessa said.

"No, clam slamming was a favorite activity while the volleyball girls showered. Any girl that was bald down there might have a fellow teammate come over and karate-chop the poor girl right in the vajayjay, and yell, 'Clam Slam!'

"If they weren't clam slamming, they were punching one another in the boobs, dirty dancing, twerking, fighting, or telling nasty stories about their boyfriends: how big or small 'it' was, how they 'did it' and all kind of other crazy stuff."

"Oh Miss Raquel...you have entirely rewritten *Gone With The Wind* for me, baby. I will never be able to look at another Southern white woman the same!" Rex burst out laughing.

After several more minutes of sharing crazy stories and laughing, Maxi came to the front desk and said, "Oh good, you have met some of the gang! So, Barbella, we are going to have Raquel direct our new Beach Volleyball program. I think this will be big-time Boom Boom for Maxi Ho Gym!"

I didn't say anything, but how did Maxi think he was going to get the city of Los Angeles to allow us to build a volleyball court on public land? I'm not sure he realized how hard that would be. It was legal to street-perform, anyone could do it, but not anyone could build volleyball courts on city parkland. This was classic Maxi behavior. You had to love his infectious passion, but at the same time, you wanted to wring his neck.

Just as I was about to say something, Maxi said, "Oh, yeah, by the way, that was Keegan, your new client on the phone. He told me to tell you that Apti would be home for Buffalo wings tonight. What is a buffalo wing? Buffalos don't have wings! That is crazy! He is very strange—*ne*?"

I threw my arms around Maxi and gave him a huge hug. "Thank you, thank you!"

"Wow, I should answer the phone more often!"

The Jail Bird Song

WHEN I GOT BACK to my apartment, I paced nervously around from one room to the next, cleaning and rearranging. The apartment was in immaculate order, but there was still no word from Apti. I tried calling him at least ten times. I didn't want to eat before I spoke to him, hoping that we could go sit somewhere outside, talk and have dinner. It was a beautiful summer evening. I decided to distract myself by watching training videos online.

Oddly, I loved to watch the craziest videos, the most extreme examples of what *not* to do in the gym. Like the Cross-Over Fit idiot with a baby strapped to his chest, pressing mega-tons of weights over his head. Or the fools that knock themselves out while weight training—literally. Or the young guys that go shirtless in public and just stand there with this stupid *I'm here, am I not amazing?* smirk on their face. I love all the girls that pass by wanting to touch them and take their picture with a real living "Muscle Adonis."

These are the young men that find their self-identity, and reason for living, by being "shredded" (cut with muscle definition), and communicate on camera with expressions like: "He is yoked (big) as fuck!" or "You get a fat pump (blood rush) doing it like that" and "Getting aesthetic as fuck keeps me motivated." In other words, focusing my entire life and reason for living on my own body and image is my life motivation. It makes *them* feel like a "man," and it made me feel sick to my stomach as a "woman."

Franco would tell me, "Barbella, most of my clients are totally body-dysmorphic. In other words, they can't see themselves as they are, as the world sees them. They can't find their own beauty. Fitness is the greatest fad in the history of mankind. Body dysmorphia is a really *negative* thing, but the business community turned it into the world's greatest money-making positive, and they are making billions of dollars perpetuating human fear and insecurity in the name of 'health and fitness.'"

I was just about to watch another training video again when the most extraordinary thing happened. I was on Giggle searching more "Crazy workout videos" when suddenly the monitor screen blinked to black and the brilliant theme song from *Star Wars* began to play. A golden robot appeared in the likeness of C-3PO and slowly walked to the center of the screen and said, "Oh Hello, I have a very special message for Serge Brantov, co-founder of Giggle!" *Oh my God,* I screamed. It was Keegan's voice. The same exact voice he used joking around with me walking today.

He continued, "Beware of the Dark Side, young master Serge. Big Brother is more ambitious than you know. Beware of the Russian Bear and the Chechen Wolf, my friend." He concluded with a wolf howl. As the music continued to its completion, the words *Beware of the Dark Side Master Serge* returned to the screen and stayed frozen for a full minute before flying off the screen with the ending musical crescendo. Keegan had successfully shut down Giggle for a full two minutes and fourteen seconds.

I sat staring at my computer screen. I was speechless, blown away by the sheer genius and tomfoolery of Keegan's caper. *My God, is Keegan a white-hat hacker?*

After I recovered from the mastery of Keegan's hoax, I realized Apti had to be with him. That was why he hadn't returned my calls. He knew I'd be waiting for him, and that I would get online and watch videos. Then I just kept repeating "Wow" over and over in my head, until I had a minor panic attack. *What if they find out Apti was involved? How could he be involved? Would they kick him out of the country? Apti doesn't know how to get behind secure digital firewalls — just how to jump over real ones!*

The phone rang. It was my mother. She was in a panic. "Did you happen to just experience your computer going black and a robot warning about the Dark Side? Is this another terrorist attack?"

I laughed. "No, Mom, this is a brilliant prank!" She babbled on about how Tonya said they experienced something like this back in England and the following day there were bombings in train stations. I assured her that this was non-related and we were not under some kind of attack. As she was about to go into round three of hysteria, I was interrupted by a call from Apti, and assured Mom we would talk tomorrow.

"Thank God you are OK!" I said, with unexpected emotion.

"I'm great, I just wanted to see if you wanted to have dinner?" he asked, as if he had been returning from a splendid vacation in the South of France.

"Yes. Of course!"

When Apti got to my apartment, I was so excited and filled with love for him. We held one another for a long time. Finally, I muttered, "I was so worried about you."

Apti explained how the police took him downtown, and the LAPD viewed his arrest as an annoyance. If they had to book and write tickets for every kid in L.A. who skated on private property, they would have to arrest most of the teenagers in Southern California. Keegan told them that he was a scientist, and showed his credentials and said that he was a colleague of Apti's father, an important research scientist assisting the Department of Defense. The police released him in fifteen minutes. On the way back to Venice, traffic was gnarly, so Keegan had plenty of time to hear Apti's version of the story.

Over our dinner, Apti excitedly shared the highlights of what Keegan had told him about Giggle in the early development days, when Serge was a graduate student at M.I.T., and his involvement and support by certain governmental security agencies. Apparently, these agencies helped fund Serge's early research project, the one that led to the creation of the Giggle search engine. The interesting part was that the CIA and NSA oversaw the initiative, which they referred to as the MDDS. The intended customers of the research were the Department of Defense and other government security organizations. In other words, Giggle was allowed to flourish to be used to assist the United States government on matters of "security."

Apti realized now that Giggle had to be in Russia, because U.S. intelligence agencies were using Giggle to harvest important information on the Russians. You can learn a lot about someone by what they search on the Internet. The troubling part for him: if the intelligence agencies were mining personal information on Russians, they were gathering personal information on Americans.

"Thanks to Keegan, I realize that my fighting Giggle on a skateboard is futile, and ultimately will only lead to me sitting in jail," Apti said. "I have reached a momentary accord, and while I am still pissed off that government agencies are spying on their citizens while maintaining they live in a democracy with individual protected rights, I will end my personal Parkour Giggle Rebellion… sometimes just knowing the truth is its own resolve!" Apt concluded with an adorable, yet devilish smile.

That was music to my ears. Maybe this would help Apti focus a little more on something more important—like me!

The RoosterCock

• • • • • • • • • • • • • • • • •

I FINALLY GOT my first female client, from my website. Her name was Selena, she but insisted I call her Sa Sa. She was from Guadalajara, but recently moved to Venice Beach after her big divorce from the "Saltillo Tile King." She brought her two young daughters, a nanny, a maid, and her handyman. She was about five-foot-four and one hundred and fifteen pounds of curves and boobs. She told me the only thing she wanted to work on was her "tushy." She wanted it to be more "Brazilian," meaning bigger and more proportionate to her breasts.

"*Él prácticamente pones un cuchillo a mi garganta para tener bustos mas grandes*. Translated, that meant: "He practically put a knife to my throat to have bigger breasts. He insisted that I have one size bigger than I wanted, *the pig!*" She was probably forty, but acted like she was twenty. She wore her hair long and pulled into a ponytail, along with tight pants and colorful low-cut tops, expensive jewelry, and super high heels.

For our first class, she wore a skin-tight t-shirt that read I LIKE GIRLS THAT LIKE GIRLS. It was an entire hour of ass-burning exercises: we ran up and down stairs, did squats and jumping squats, ballet barre work, jogging, and resistance training. Selena seemed happy in our sessions, but she seemed to get more and more sexually provocative with her comments. First, she touched my arm, then my waist, and then spanked me on the butt, saying, "Wish I could have *pompis* like yours."

At first, I didn't notice her comments as strange, but one day after a session, Vanessa said: "I thought she was going to try to muff-dive you right here on the gym floor when you two were stretching!"

"Honey that little Sa Sa Miranda wants to wear *your fruit* up on top of her face!" Rex said, laughing.

"I think she is hot. Can I watch?" Halo offered.

But I felt really uncomfortable. I talked to the gang about it, they said, "Don't worry about it! This happens all the time." Halo said, "I wish I had a dollar for every time one of my clients said something sexually suggestive. I'd be rich as a sheik!"

"I know you would want to be a sheik, so you can *pop* that genie right out the bottle and do—*nasty things*—in the harem tent, have your own little Desert Storm, you sick SEAL!"

"Rex, you are probably the only *registered* sexual offender in Compton!"

"No baby, we don't need a registry to know who is fucking who in the hood!"

"Oh yeah? I can spot a sexual predator from twelve city blocks," Vanessa chirped.

"Miss NYC, you couldn't tell the difference between a sexual predator and a sexual *pretender*. Besides, I bet they could shoot the sequel to *Frozen* in your coochie, it is so dormant. In fact, you may be the *evidence* that we are heading to the next ice age!"

"Bar, honey, just tell Sa Sa on your next session, about your *boyfriend*, and she will stop flirting! And as for you, Rex, see *you* next Tuesday!"

Before anyone could ask what that meant, I saw Keegan arrive.

Keegan came into the gym and I noticed he was wearing a t-shirt that said, I'M NOT A HACKER, I'M A SECURITY PROFESSIONAL! I broke out laughing, and ran over and gave him a huge hug and a big smack on the cheek that made him turn bright red. And I thanked him repeatedly for helping Apti.

During our cardio walk along the beach, Keegan told me all about rescuing Apti from the LAPD. He also went on and on about the nefarious dark forces that abound in the federal "security agencies" in the name of "protecting" the American people. I found the subject overwhelming and gave him new exercises to try to slow him down. After I steered him away from the dark shadowy forces, he told me how much he enjoyed meeting Apti.

"The kid has a real intensity that I like. You know, he doesn't pretend. He is so real. He's had to deal with a lot in life for such a young guy."

"Yeah, I am really lucky to be in a relationship with such an honest guy."

"I know he is *really* crazy about you. It must suck that he is already engaged to be married back in Chechnya."

"What?"

"He didn't tell you?"

"Tell me *what?*"

"Well, I got the impression that his father was back in Chechnya to finalize plans for Apti to marry, you know, an arranged-marriage sort of thing."

I didn't say it out loud, but I thought, *I'll kill him.*

• • •

After the gym had cleared out later that day, Maxi came to the front desk screaming and cursing in Korean. We knew the financial situation was bad, but we didn't realize how bad. "How the hell am I supposed to run a business in this country? The bank says that now I have two weeks to pay them forty thousand or bye-bye Maxi Ho Gym!"

Of course, any one of us would happily give Maxi the money, but none of us had any. We were all just getting by. I think Raquel was the most disturbed because she had come all the way from Alabama for her summer internship.

"What are you going to do, Miss Purple Haze, if we shut down?" Rex asked with genuine concern.

"Work on my love life and get a better tan!"

"Don't worry, Maxi, it will work out. It always does!" I said, trying to be upbeat.

"You kids don't understand. This is all I have," Maxi said, almost in tears.

Rex stepped up and cleared his throat. In a Southern, Frederick Douglass statesman-like voice, he declared, "Now my friends, the news we face may appear bleak, but I *glory* in the conflict, that I may hereafter enjoy the *victory*, because I know that *victory* is certain. We will continue, for the sake of our brethren, we *lift up* our voices on their behalf; and struggle in their ranks for the emancipation that *shall yet be achieved*. Can I have an *amen*?"

"Amen," we all said.

"Now, that you have pledged your devotion to the cause and we are all resolute in our joined purpose, let us march together to the RoosterCock and drink to our certain victory! We *shall* overcome!"

Maxi agreed. "OK, OK, let's go make Disco Boom Boom!"

"To the Cock!" Rex clapped his hands firmly as the trumpet call, and we all skipped along with him to his alma mater, the RoosterCock Bar.

I had never been to a gay bar. Actually, I had never been to a bar of any kind.

Apti joined us, but I kept my distance. I didn't want to make a big deal out of it tonight, when we were all trying to feel better and support Maxi, but I was shoe-throwing-mad underneath it all.

Apti and I were the only trainers under twenty-one. Because we were a big group and drinks were being sent to the table, no one really asked our age. The music was loud techno; the lighting was dark. We sat in the back by the pool table. At this time of day, it was pretty tame, full of mostly older guys who looked retired but still in good shape. Everyone was tan, looked like they went to gyms, and many of the younger guys didn't wear shirts. I recognized several of the guys from our gym, and they were really sweet to us and sent over rounds of shots that they called the "Three Wise Men: Jack, Jim, & José."

When the drinks came, everyone lifted their shot glass and Rex toasted, "To the Three Wise Men: Maxi, Plato and Halo, and all the other hoes in the gym!" The drink burned my throat and flushed my face. I began to feel like I was part of the beat of the music, the laughter, and the energy in the room. My sharp anger toward Apti was beginning to slightly dull. Our clients sent another round, and then another, and then another.

Rex was dancing. I mean, really dancing, and everyone in the room was fixated on his body. He danced over to the table and pulled me up. I thought I would die, but then something in my gut said, "Shut up, girl, and dance." Or maybe Rex said it. Anyway, I danced. I surrendered to the beat and moved with it and allowed everything else in the world to leave my mind. I closed my eyes and I didn't have a mind, just a body and warm feelings. I felt someone touching me, dancing with me, and I opened my eyes. It was Apti. His eyes were closed and he looked like an angel. I grabbed his face and pulled him toward me. I wanted to slap him violently for lying to me. Instead, I gave him a passionate kiss. There was nothing else in the world. He pulled me into his arms and we stood still together on the dance floor, with nothing but our heavy breath and our hearts beating together.

After our dance, the bar filled quickly and things started getting crazy. Halo and Vanessa were dancing together, very sexy. Raquel and Franco were kissing back at the table. Plato and Apti started some kind of Sufi whirling-dervish circular movement on the dance floor and others joined. They locked arms, and added people, after a few minutes they formed a dancing prayer circle and started chanting, "We are one—we are one—we are one…"

I went into the ladies' room but found more men than women. When I opened the stall door, I found a young lanky white guy with long hair and a tall, beautiful drag queen who looked like Marilyn Monroe with platinum blonde and pink hair snorting cocaine. They invited me to join them. I politely moved on to the next stall where I found a trans man adjusting his "business." I went back to the first stall and said, "Do you mind if I tinkle?" They broke out laughing and the drag queen said, "Of course not, darling, we are all queens here. Your throne awaits."

I had to *really* go and I was drunk, so I just sat down and did what I had to do. The drag queen said, "Where are my manners? Sweetness, this is my friend Sky and my name is Magnolia Thunder Twat." She passed a tiny spoon and put it in my nostril. "Cover your other nostril and snort this!" I don't know why, but I did as she instructed. They both laughed at my goofy expression and began to leave the stall. Then Magnolia stopped and turned. "Welcome to the tea party, baby!" They shut the door and laughed like wicked aunts. The music was so loud and the spotlight from the track lights on the ceiling made an interesting pattern on the stainless door. I just sat there and stared at my reflection in the light. For just a moment, I experienced myself as beautiful in that light. I sat motionless and listened to the music. That is, until I heard knocks on the stall door. "Come on, honey, this isn't your seaside condo!"

When I left the bathroom, I felt invincible. I strutted through the crowd of men to our table and saw that everyone was dancing, or on the back patio drinking and talking. Apti was still doing his whirling-dervish thing, so I walked around and looked at people. I felt very sensual and attractive. That was a very different feeling for me. The boys were so sweet: "Oh, baby, you are so hot... I love your eyes, you have green tiger eyes... girl, I would die for those plump hot lips... what I wouldn't do to have thick, long, beautiful hair... Girl, your arms are buffer than mine!"

I saw Rex at the bar holding court. He always found a way to connect and put folks at ease. As I watched him, I thought, *Is it only people who have had to overcome a deep level of personal pain in their lives? Can anyone have the same level of empathy?* I felt so much love for him and I wanted to tell him so. But he turned toward the door with a man I recognized as a visiting artist from Mexico.

The bar was packed now, wall-to-wall. I made my way over to where Vanessa was standing watching a very interesting guy play pool. He was tall and muscular, very masculine in ripped blue jeans and black biker boots. The most striking feature about his appearance was his numerous body piercings: his nipples, his navel, and his ears had about ten studs each.

Without thinking I belted out, "Wow, where don't you have a piercing?" He flashed me a naughty and inviting smile, as if to say, *Come here, Little Red Riding Hood.*

"Well, would you like to see?"

"Why yes, yes we would!" Vanessa blurted.

After he dropped the eight ball in the corner pocket, with a loud thud, he took us down the dark bathroom hallway and stopped in front of the cigarette machine for some light. There he turned around and without hesitation, unzipped his jeans and pulled out his big, thick rooster cock. Vanessa and I both screamed at the same time.

His thingy had what was referred to as a "Prince Albert": a thick silver metal ring embedded into the tip. It had a chain that attached his "prince" to his navel.

I was fascinated with the sculptural aspect of the ensemble, but Vanessa was having a panic attack. "Oh my God! What happens when it gets happy?" The guy smirked, stowed it back in his tight jeans, and turned and went back down the hall and into the bar without a word.

Meanwhile, back at our table, Plato and Maxi had gotten into a serious philosophical conversation. I looked over at the bar and saw my client, Sa Sa, with a new hairstyle—bleached blonde hair slicked back as if she were a nineteenth-century Englishman—and her hands were all over Raquel. She acted as if she didn't see me. Franco was arguing with some big guy who said something nasty to him about kissing Raquel on the dance floor. I knew we had to get him out of there before Franco went "Flatbush" on him.

I grabbed Franco. "Come here, I need to talk to you!" Then I grabbed Apti, who was in some kind of tequila trance on the dance floor, and walked him directly out the front door. I didn't realize how drunk we were until I got outside and heard the sound of the ocean and smelled the salty air. I felt as if I had been in an alternate reality—a sensual bonfire, in a strangely entertaining male carnival, a gay Fellini movie.

Franco said good night and took off. I took a deep breath and asked Apti if he wanted to spend the night at my place.

He started mumbling in Chechen and then replied, "Yes."

"OK, but first, we have to talk about something…"

"Yes, OK."

"Is it true that you are engaged to be married back in Chechnya?"

"No—*absolutely*—not!"

"Why are you telling me a lie?"

"I am *not* telling you a lie!"

"Then, why did Keegan tell me that your father returned to Chechnya to arrange your marriage? You told me that he returned to care for your *sick grandmother*—you are a liar!"

"My grandmother *is sick* and my father did return to take care of her. It's true, he wants me to marry a Chechen girl— *and*— he wants to find someone he can 'arrange' for me, that is what I told Keegan… but, you see, *I don't want to marry a Chechen girl*, because I am *in love with you*. Don't you understand, *crazy girl*, my father left Venice before I met you?"

Before I could jump into his arms and tell him how much I loved him, Apti threw his head forward and vomited ferociously on the street. From behind, I heard Maxi and Plato laughing.

"Jackson Pollock would be proud!" Plato said, in his usual ironic manner.

"So much for the Three Wise Men!" I responded, helping Apti stand-up.

"Don't ever underestimate the importance of a wise man," Plato said, in a whisper, but no one was listening.

The Radiant Child

• • • • • • • • • • • • • • • •

THE NEXT MORNING, I woke up with Apti in my arms. The sun poured generously into my bedroom window and while my head felt like a team of mules had taken turns stepping on me, I felt amazing. I took a deep breath and just felt Apti's naked body in my arms. My mind replayed moments of our passion, our kisses, and our exploration of one another. I worried that Apti would have a problem with us making love before marriage and when I asked him before we fell asleep if he felt OK about what we did, he said, "Who am I to argue with the beauty of God's creation!"

I was in no hurry to wake him, or to face the gym this morning. I just lay there thinking about Maxi's announcement; it seemed pretty obvious that the gym would have to close. I thought, *At least I had my trainer certification and some experience. I could always get a part-time job somewhere and do personal training on the side.*

I decided to stop thinking about the future and focus on the beauty of the moment. I put on a robe and decided that this was the morning that I would conquer Sophie's fancy French coffee maker, and make Apti a banana and honey crêpe. After everything looked perfect on the tray, I decided to be silly and bring Apti breakfast in bed naked, adding a flower behind my ear, and sing a funny little wake-up song.

I didn't hear the front door unlock as I loaded my tray for the big breakfast surprise, and at precisely the moment that I was in front of the front door, it opened widely, and I froze. First, I saw a large black suitcase, followed by a cheerful "Bon jour!" greeting from Sophie, and Claude. At that moment, Apti walked out calling my name, still thinking I was in the kitchen, completely oblivious, and naked, trying to amuse me by hanging a towel over his Mister Happy as it stood at full attention.

Claude laughed. "Sophie, I feel like we are overdressed, *n'est-ce pas!*" Sophie looked at Apti and added slyly, "Well, I see you have come to the apartment for a visit!" Apti turned red and excused himself, returning to the bedroom. Mortified, I retrieved my robe.

After Sophie and Claude made some more jokes to lighten the mood, Apti came out and ate his crêpe, and I made everyone coffee. Sophie exclaimed, "Well, *Cherie*, I just came home to get a few things and we have an early plane to catch. We are off to Spain and Morocco!"

"You two should come to New Caledonia sometime and stay on the ranch. I am sure you would enjoy it!" Claude warmly said.

We agreed we would love it, but doubted that we would have enough money anytime in the near future to visit. Sophie gathered her things.

"Well, Cherie, I am so pleased that you have settled in and are enjoying the apartment. You take care and give your Daddy a big hug for me."

"Will do! Sorry for the shocking greeting when you arrived…"

"Maybe shocking for you kids. For us, a pleasure to know that love is in the air!"

• • •

When I got to the gym, Plato was cleaning, and in an oddly good mood, whistling and acting really strange. I ignored him and concentrated on Vanessa, whom I thought might actually be dead. She was on the floor of her yoga studio and not moving or breathing. I ran in and shook her shoulders.

Her eyes popped open. "What, are you trying to give me a *freakin* heart attack?"

I apologized profusely and told me that she hadn't sleep more than an hour last night. She and Halo stayed at the RoosterCock until it closed, partying with the boys, and ended up over at his place, and one thing led to another, and, well…

Maxi came into the studio with a dark energy cloud swirling around him and dramatically announced, "We will close for business, effective tomorrow."

If he didn't do that, he explained, he wouldn't be able to keep the place open for two more weeks to give everyone time to look for other jobs. He told me to call the entire staff for a general meeting after lunch, to announce the official closing of Maxi Ho Gym. Something about the words "official closing" made me really upset and I had to fight back bursting out in tears. I don't know if it was the hangover, lack of sleep, or the fact that Apti and I made love, but I was very emotional—raw. Maxi also told me to make signs to put on both doors for our members to announce the closing.

Plato stopped his janitorial duties and walked over to say. "Let's hold off until tomorrow on the signs. It might just make people more upset!" I agreed, and started the dreadful task of calling everyone. Mom called me on my mobile phone, and I ignored it. Then I received a text: *Bar, I need to see you today. Can you have lunch?* There couldn't have been a worse day, but she had *never* in my entire life said, "I *need to see you!*" I remembered her saying something about "needing to have some girl talk" the other day when she ran into Dad and I at the apartment. After I reached all the gym staff about the meeting, I called Mom and agreed to lunch.

As Mom pulled up in front of the gym, Rex arrived. He swung open the door of her car on the passenger side before I could get there and enthusiastically said, "Oh Lord, you must be Little Miss Jackie O's mommy?" It startled my mom, because she had never met Rex and didn't know who "Little Miss Jackie O" was. She screamed like a siren and reached inside her handbag, then aimed her Mace directly at his face and started screaming, "I don't have any money!" I ran up to the car before she could spray him and tried to calm her down. I don't know who was more freaked out, Rex or Mom!

After I formally introduced Rex, now embarrassed to have upset Mom, and I explained the Jackie O reference, she was sweet as a kitten and invited him over for dinner sometime. If Mom liked someone, she always said, "Come over sometime and have dinner with us." It was definitely something she picked up in her Midwest childhood. For Mom, all matters of family, friends or life challenges should be dealt with calmly and lovingly over a good meal.

When I got in the car, she could sense something different about me, and I could tell something was upsetting her. We decided to head to Abbot Kinney Boulevard. Mom said it was kind of a special occasion, so she was taking me to Laurent's, a French-Californian restaurant. That piqued my interest. I had never eaten there. If we ate out, it was usually at places where Mom or Dad knew the owners from the gym. This may have been the first time she took me to a really nice restaurant, just the two of us. It was the kind of place where the sauce on the plate looked like art, and the food was adorned with unusual vegetables and brightly colored edible flowers for color and texture.

We ordered, and neither of us seemed in a rush to discuss the point of our dining together. It was clear to both of us that this was lovely and we wanted that feeling to last as long as possible. Mom inquired about Apti. The only words I could manage to find was, "He is great!" She seemed disappointed by my brevity, so I mustered up, "We are really getting closer."

Mom asked about how training was going and I told her about Keegan, the reluctant genius, and Sa Sa, the heat-seeking hoochie mama, which made her laugh. It was nice to see her laugh. Usually, she seemed really stressed out and tired from flying. Her jewelry business added even more stress. After the waiter cleared the plates, Mom seemed to get really pensive, the look she gets when she has to say something that is emotionally complicated. Not unlike the time we spoke about my involuntary departure for Miss Palmer's School. She always struggled to find the right words.

"Bar, there is something I need to talk to you about," she said right as the waiter brought our entrees.

The food was gorgeous. It was the prettiest chicken breast I had ever seen in my life. I told Mom, "My God, some poor chicken forfeited her breast for my dining pleasure... thank you, thank you!" I thought my comment would make Mom smile, but instead, tears streamed down her face.

Mom apologizing for being so emotional and after she pulled it together, she said, "Bar honey, I have breast cancer!"

Tears instantly filled my eyes. The waiter came to the table and said, "Is everything prepared to your satisfaction?" I started laughing and said, "Yes, it's so good, it's bringing us to tears!" My comment made us both laugh out loud, and made our very careful waiter nervously excuse himself.

Mom explained that her oncologist said that her cancer was Stage Two, and that it was *treatable*, that it was *contained*, and that she should be fine after treatment. The doctor recommended the removal of both of her breasts, to err on the safe side.

I looked at my chicken breast and lost all desire to eat. I instinctively reached over the table for Mom's hand. Her lovely long fingers wrapped around my hand and there was so much love exchanged in that single touch that it was hard for me to express to her what I was feeling in words. She smiled and took a deep breath. "I'm going to be fine, darling."

"Does Dad know?"

"Darling, why would I tell your father?"

"Because he is *my father* and I think he should know!"

"I'm not ready to talk about this with anyone else right now, OK darling?"

"Mom, you are going to have to let all that anger go sometime, especially now."

"I know, darling, I know. It will all work out."

• • •

In spite of drinking four cups of coffee at the restaurant, the emotional weight of Mom's news, my breakthrough with Apti, and the gym closing—which I couldn't manage to share with Mom—and a wicked "Wise Men" hangover, I wanted to skip work and lay on the beach in a fetal position.

But to the gym I went. The first person I saw outside was Halo. He looked horrible. I had only seen him look ruggedly fit and ready for action. "Barbella, can I talk to you for a second?" he asked, desperately.

"Can it wait? I really have to go in and organize the meeting."

"I really have to ask you something quickly!"

I walked over. "What's up?"

His face was filled with anxiety and then he just jumped, like he was on one of his missions, and said, "Barbella, last night, well I got really smashed and Vanessa and I stayed way too long at that bar…"

I stopped him and said, "I know, no big deal, you and Vanessa hooked up. Life goes on. You don't have to marry the woman. Relax!"

He looked embarrassed, like he was going to cry and said, "No, that is the thing, you see, Vanessa isn't a woman entirely…"

I couldn't help myself and I roared with laughter and without thinking blurted out, "Vanessa is a chick with a dick?" That was all I needed to make a perfectly bizarre day, even stranger. "You saw it?"

"Well… I felt it more than saw it… Does that mean I am gay?" Halo asked, still in shock.

"Oh, please, it just means you had a crazy, drunken adventure. At ease, soldier, this is top-secret classified information—*and will stay that way*. Dismissed!"

Halo, looking much relieved, snapped to attention and gave a crisp, and straight salute. "Ma'am, yes ma'am!"

Inside the gym, the first thing I heard was Vanessa telling Rex, "Oh my God, my ass is killing me!"

"Oh yes, you definitely had your cha cha on last night, sista, with all that dancing!"

I went to Plato, who was setting up the folding chairs for the meeting. He greeted me as usual. "Hello, darling girl!"

I helped him set up the remaining chairs and then went to find Maxi to tell him we were ready. I found Maxi in his office. He was crying. He obviously had not slept and was still drinking some kind of Korean rice wine and singing along to a Korean folk song. I hugged him. He told me the song was the most beautiful and sad song that he knew. He started translating it as the lovely girl sang:

> *Man's heart is like water streaming downhill;*
> *Woman's heart is well water—so deep and still.*
>
> *Young men's love is like pinecones seeming sound,*
> *But when the wind blows, they fall to the ground.*
>
> *Birds in the morning sing simply to eat;*
> *Birds in the evening sing for love sweet.*
>
> *When man has attained to the age of a score,*
> *The mind of a woman should be his love.*
>
> *The trees and the flowers will bloom for aye,*
> *But the glories of youth will soon fade away.*

I fetched him some coffee and told him that everything was ready. He said he was too drunk and asked me to make the announcement. I didn't think that was appropriate, so I told him I would ask Plato. He thought that was a great idea.

"Plato is a genius," he said, and then put his head down on his desk, crying harder. I made him drink more coffee and went to find Plato. He was in an almost inappropriately great mood and said he would be happy to make the announcement!

This day simply *could not* get any stranger.

After everyone arrived and was seated, we brought Maxi out to the gym and everyone stood up and gave him a standing ovation and chanted, "Maxi, Maxi, Maxi," which made him start crying again. I placed him on the front row, so he could see Plato. Plato had put on a sports jacket he borrowed from the lost-and-found box, along with a t-shirt a Giggle member gave him that read STAY CALM AND CODE ON. Plato cleared his throat, looked lovingly toward Maxi, surveyed the gang for a moment, and began to speak:

"My dear friends, as many of you know by now, Maxi has had to make a very difficult and painful decision to close the gym..."

You could hear physical reactions in the room: people moving in their chairs, sighs that conveyed disappointment, and several sniffling noses.

"The gym is closing, not because you have performed your jobs poorly, nor that our members didn't prosper from your efforts to bring them improved fitness and health. I think we all know that *everyone* did the very best they could to bring *true excellence*."

Everyone cheered and applauded.

"No, the reason the Maxi Ho Gym must close is based entirely on a financial decision, a decision made in some dim fluorescent light-stained cubicle in a golden-mirrored skyscraper far from Venice Beach, by an indifferent analyst that has earmarked our loan as no longer profitable for their bank."

Everyone yelled, "Boo!"

"But the financial realities of this world do not concern us today, my friends. We have profited a much greater return than money. We are the beneficiaries of something much greater. We have received the gift of friendship, human kindness, and love.

"I ask you to think for a moment about where you were in your life a few short months ago and ask yourself, am I a better person today? Has this group of people, which you have come to know and love, not enriched your life? Are we not a group that most would call odd, perhaps even strange, and yet, have we not found a safe place to be ourselves and to flourish?

"And finally, did this not all begin with effort of one man? Isn't it safe to say that Mr. Henry Ho, all those years ago when he arrived to Los Angeles from Korea in search of a better life for himself and his family, contributed and touched so many people's lives with a simple philosophical idea—*be kind to every living human being*.

"Mr. Ho's wealth didn't come from multiple units of grocery stores; it came from one small store, in a poor neighborhood, where he gave his compassion, kindness, and more of his profits to others than he kept for himself. I believe his adopted son, Maximilian Ho, has done a tremendous job to continuing this tradition."

Everyone stood and applauded thunderously, again chanting, "Maxi, Maxi, Maxi!"

"Before I conclude, I would like to share a very special and personal story with you. I apologize in advance if it is a bit long and tiresome, but I feel sure you will appreciate the significance by the conclusion.

"First, I have to ask you if you are familiar with the American painter Jean-Michel Basquiat?"

Rex spoke up. "Yes, I am. He was the first African-American painter in the world to gain international prominence; he was on the art scene in the Eighties. He was from Vanessa's hometown of Brooklyn, and hung out with Andy Warhol. I saw one of his paintings recently at the Museum of Contemporary Art in Los Angeles!"

"Yes, that is correct," Plato, said. "He had an extraordinary rise in the international art scene, making a tremendous splash, and very sadly died when he was only twenty-eight years old, due to a drug overdose.

"In 1977, while he was still a young student, he and a friend started doing graffiti art around New York. They used the tag name SAMO. After a couple of years, Basquiat stopped graffiti art and started putting his work on canvas when a very successful art gallery owner gave him a large studio space in her gallery's basement, and paid for his canvas and paint. In 1981, the first night of his New York City opening in her gallery, they sold every painting, and he made two hundred thousand dollars.

"In 1984, my lovely wife Elizabeth and I were living in West Hollywood. I just landed my job teaching philosophy at UCLA and Elizabeth was painting full-time in her studio. She told me about this amazing young painter from New York City that was opening at the Cogen Art Gallery on Robertson Boulevard and insisted we go. I absolutely made a fuss about going. I had too much to do, too many papers to grade, maybe we could go later in the week. She would have nothing to do with my excuses and I went kicking and screaming...

"Until I walked in the door and saw what was on the gallery walls. I maneuvered my way through the crowd, and stood in front of a work entitled *Hollywood Africans 1940* painted mostly in primary colors, anchored by graphic words randomly placed, and three figurative faces, one entitled *self-portrait as a heel #3*. My brain picked out words from the painting: *200 yen, Gangsterism, Paw Paw, Sugar Cane,* and my favorite, '*What is Bwana?*' I was in an aesthetic dream state and I knew I was in the company of a genius.

"The spell was broken when a young man, about twenty-two years old, with amazing hair shooting from his head like thick braids of squid-ink pasta, and sensitive eyes, inquisitively asked me, 'So what do you think?' I knew it was Jean-Michel. I didn't know what to say. I tripped mentally and struggled to regain my composure. Finally, I managed an enthusiastic declarative statement: 'Well, it's worth more than two hundred yen!" He seemed to be amused and shook my hand and with a big smirk and responded by saying, 'Bet your white Sambo ass!' He turned, and walked back into the crowd of adoring admirers and Hollywood hipsters.

"After the opening, I learned that Basquiat was living in an old building that used to be an art gallery in Venice Beach for another year to work on a second show at the Cogen Gallery before he returned to New York. His studio was on Market Street. It was at Fifty-Six Market Street to be exact, across the street from a certain Ho Grocery Company at Fifty-Four Market Street. Folks around here say that on more than one occasion, Jean-Michel would bang on Mr. Ho's door after he was closed and ask for groceries or something he could use for art supplies—a sheet of plywood, old shipping crates, old doors, window frames—and he would give Mr. Ho drawings to 'pay' for these items. Mr. Ho thought he was just another unfortunate homeless kid living on the streets trying to escape an abusive father, or mother addicted to crack.

"Mr. Ho happily took the strange drawings with big crowns, words scratched through, skulls, references to jazz artists, and put them in a bottom drawer in the back of the store in his apartment, where he kept all the nice things people gave him to say thank you for his kindness."

Rex suddenly stood up and gasped, "Oh Lord, like the drawing we saw in your apartment when Maxi was giving us a tour... like the one Maxi threw away, with the crown and Satchmo?"

"Precisely, like the one Maxi threw in the garbage!

"Last night, after our evening at the RoosterCock, I couldn't sleep and decided to clean out junk from the drawers in my apartment... while I was cleaning up, I happened to stumble upon a drawer full of small drawings on paper, forty to be exact... all original Basquiat drawings. I think it is fair to say, given the current price of a Basquiat drawing, they are probably worth more than Maxi's entire bank debt."

Everyone was quiet.

Then Maxi jumped up and screamed, *"Thank you, God.* Thank you, Mr. Ho. Thank you Mr. Basket. Thank you, Plato. Now, we can stay and make more Ho Gym Boom Boom!"

Everyone cheered and chanted, "Maxi, Maxi, Maxi."

Plato raised his arms to get the attention of the gang and everyone calmed down to let him continue.

"There is one more part to the story, friends. The discovery of the drawings caused me to be haunted by the memory of my lovely wife Elizabeth, and the Basquiat Art Opening we attended together many years ago. I considered the words I told him, 'It's worth more than two hundred yen!' And, his great response, "You bet your white Sambo ass!" I laughed and I cried remembering how beautiful Elizabeth looked that evening in her tight-fitting red dress and black stiletto heels. She looked like an Italian movie star.

"Restless, I decided to clean out the back storage closet in Juicy. It was filled with trash, old signs, lumber, brooms, mop handles, and a large framed canvas in the very back covered with a dirty old sheet. It was too large for me to carry, so I dragged it out slowly by pulling it on its side. When I uncovered it, turned it around and leaned it against the wall, what I saw screamed off the canvas: I recognized the explosion of random words, rich color, and the specific style could only be the work of Jean-Michel Basquiat.

"As I stared at the painting, at the top in large black, thick letters he painted *Art Opening*, with the word Art crossed through. The painting was mostly bright-marigold colored, with splashes of sky blue, with a spattering of words scrambled over the canvas. Off-center, on the right side of the canvas, was the figure of a woman wearing a red dress and exaggerated black stiletto shoes with 'Liz,' 'Lizzie,' and 'Elizabeth' printed beside her hips. My eyes scanned the work to identify the words dancing around the canvas, like improvisational trills of a youthful horn player: *Richie Rich, Lost Angeles, Blind leading blind, Famous Kid*—with the F painted over—*Wall Street, White Sambo*, and in big letters at the bottom, the exact words that I nervously told him that evening at the gallery, *'It's definitely worth more than 200 yen.'*

"In the middle of the canvas was the image of an Asian man with round glasses and below it was printed, 'SAMO HO' with the word 'SAMO' crossed through. I stood for at least an hour staring and crying into the canvas, wishing somehow to have them all back with me: Elizabeth, my lovely daughter, Jean-Michel, and Mr. Ho."

Plato stopped speaking and everyone remained silent, as Halo and Rex brought the painting in front of the room and slowly took the sheet off the work.

"Isn't it perfect?" Plato asked.

Everyone in the room went wild with applause.

"Well, my friends, I think it is safe to say, Maxi, you *really* don't have to worry about closing the gym! The last original Basquiat oil painting to sell at auction, at Christie's, was called *Dust Heads 1982*, and it sold for forty-eight-point-four million dollars."

Everyone jumped up and down, dancing, screaming, and making noise. Maxi jumped atop of his chair and yelled, "OK, people, let's party like it's 1982!"

Five

Nine Months Later

• • • • • •

LIFE CAN BE so strange. One minute you are facing the edge of a cliff, and the next you have sprouted wings and are taking flight. Needless to say, Plato's discovery brought about numerous changes for the gang and the Ho Gym.

Maxi contacted Christie's and arranged for the work to be authenticated. Then he released the painting for auction. After taxes and auction fees, the forty Basquiat drawings brought enough money to pay off the gym's bank loan. The painting entitled *Art Opening 1982* fetched forty million dollars at auction, slightly less than expected because it was sold so quickly without advance promotion. After taxes and auction fees, the painting netted Maxi just under twenty-two million dollars. In the meantime, Ho Gym continued to run as before.

Maxi insisted that we keep the discovery on the down low, but within two weeks, reporters from the *Los Angeles Times* got wind of "The Lost Venice Beach Basquiat" and it brought a whirlwind of interest to our little gym and the Ho family story. Maxi said this was the third most important Korean event in American history: The Rodney King Riots and the Korean store owners; Psy's hit "Gangnam Style"; and the humble Korean grocery store owner who had been given major art treasures by a world-famous artist—treasures that sat for more than two decades before being discovered in the storage closet of a gym.

The first thing Maxi did when he received payment was to invite all of the original trainers and Plato to dinner to say thank you. We went to a BBQ restaurant in Koreatown named Gwang Lee that had a nice private room. It was so much fun. Apti had never eaten Korean food and loved the spicy dishes. He used long metal chopsticks to enjoy his *kimchi* and *gogigui*. We drank *soju*, a wickedly strong rice wine that was like Japanese sake. Halo sat opposite Vanessa and there was an unsettling tension between them. After we all laughed and joked about the crazy last several months, Maxi said he had a special announcement for everyone.

Rex said, "Oh Lord, please don't tell us you found another painting. My little heart couldn't stand it!" Everyone laughed, but Maxi's face was uncharacteristically serious.

"So, my friends, we have a Korean saying, '*Go-saeng Ggeut-eh naki eun-da.*' It means, 'At the end of hardship comes happiness.' I know that things have not always been easy. I also realize how much you each gave to making Ho Gym a success. Yes, Ho Gym was a success even though the bank wanted to close us down.

"Even my friend Renzo, Barbella's daddy, told me long ago, 'Without free weights, machines, parking, and showers you're gonna be in deep shit!' But, you all had the courage to believe in me and make big-time *pali pali* Boom Boom!"

Everyone raised his or her soju cup. "To *pali pali* Boom Boom!"

Maxi raised his hands after they drank. "Sorry, sorry, almost forgot. One more thing… I have prepared a small thank-you." Maxi pulled some envelopes with our names printed on the outside and passed them out. "It is rather boring and doesn't adequately tell you how much I appreciate you all…"

In Korean culture, you never open a gift right away, but we all simultaneously ripped open the envelopes. The table was so quiet; you could only hear the sound of a waiter outside cursing in Korean.

Everyone at the table started to cry, laugh, and thank Maxi. He had given each founding trainer, and me, a check for one million dollars. Plato had been given two million. He sighed deeply. His eyes were glassy. "Unnecessary," he said, "but thank you, dear man, thank you!"

I didn't want to but I couldn't stop thinking about the money. *My God, what did that mean? Was I rich? What should I do with it?* I felt like going to the bank after we finished dinner and depositing it. I felt so vulnerable. I had never had any amount of money. *Should I invest it? Should I buy something for my mom?* I was utterly overwhelmed.

Apti seemed slightly detached from his gift. I think for him, money was an annoying reality that he didn't really care about. He seemed to value how God worked or did not work through people, and I know he deeply appreciated Maxi's generosity and kindness.

Maxi hit his glass with a metal chopstick to get everyone's attention.

"I hope that this gift will not take you away from the gym. I still need you! In fact, I am going to open up my dream gym. I'm already working with an architect." He pronounced the word ar-*chee*-techt, and we all laughed and said, "Are-*key*-tekt!" He said it was a "top secret" and he would show us the design later. He intended to move the current gym temporarily down the street until the new building was ready for business. He assured us the new gym would be Boom Boom crazy cool, big-time Maxi Ho Gangnam style!

The Fine Line

● ● ● ● ● ● ● ● ● ● ● ● ●

WE GROW UP in the United States thinking that money, physical beauty, and fame brings us happiness. We think it is what we should all strive for. I already knew that a beautiful body and muscles don't make a person smart, interesting, kind, or spiritually nourished. I had been around plenty of "famous" people, and knew what a joke that was. Some of the most neurotic, messed-up people I had been around in my entire life were so-called Hollywood stars. Rex called the whole cultural mess "Hollywood Syndrome." He would say, "Child, everyone wants to be rich and *fabulous*. I wish the world could see just how manufactured all this Hollywood jive shit is. Man, they should rename the place 'Swinging Dick Peckerwood La La Land'—that would be more honest!"

Sure, the Maxi money was great to have, don't get me wrong, and it gave us some opportunities that we wouldn't have had, as easily or quickly. But there was some other stuff that came with it. The first one to feel the sting was Rex.

Rex went home to visit his mom in Compton, to surprise her with a fat check so that she could buy herself a nice little bungalow in Santa Monica and get out of "The Hood." She was so excited when she opened her gift; she cried tears of joy and thanked "the baby Jesus" repeatedly. Rex used the other half of the money toward finishing his English degree in creative writing, and to buy a small condo. After he enrolled and began school part-time, he went to visit his mother to help her with the new home search.

It seems that his stepfather, Bob Peoples, had been released from jail and used her money as collateral to invest it in an old church, right in the middle of Compton, where he intended to administer the "Word of God" to the deserving and needing folks of Compton. "In prison, I found Jesus and have been saved. We can't turn our back on our own community," Bob Peoples told Rex's mom, and she later told Rex, as he poured more bourbon to go with his eggs and bacon.

I truly worried that Rex was going to murder him. Rex asked me to go with him to the Compton Church of Christ, to hear the esteemed Reverend Bob Peoples preach on Sunday. "Baby, this shit is going to stop right now, once and for all," Rex told me.

We got to the church on Sunday morning right in the middle of his stepfather's sermon. Bob Peoples was wearing a new pin-striped suit. He held a handkerchief in his hand and waved it from time to time to punctuate the words "Praise God!" His sermon was on morality and what he called the "fine line."

"Jesus understood the *fine line*... He knew that there would be those people that don't see you doing God's work, don't understand your message of love... don't understand your compassion, and are going to think you just trying to get something from them..."

"Praise God," the congregation said.

"Jesus understood the fine line... Brothers and sisters, he understood that in this life other people will try to bring you harm, they will manipulate you, they will lie to you, and they will be tempted daily by the devil... the fine line, brothers and sisters, is our power to choose. God gave us *free will*: in the face of this world's hardships and pain, we can chose to love, and choose to find compassion and forgiveness. And from this place of power—the power to choose compassion—we are one with God."

"Praise God," the congregation said.

"Brothers and sisters, this is when we take a moment to recognize another fine line—giving! Yes, brothers and sisters, we don't want to live in a world of meaningless materialism, but *we got to pay to pray* in the real world… just as Jesus paid with his life, so must we *pay* to have a house to worship his name—Praise God."

"Praise God," the congregation said.

Rex was moving from side to side and crossing and uncrossing his legs. As the church organ begin to play, ushers came around with large brass contribution plates. The congregation fell into silence.

Rex stood and walked directly to the front and stood facing the congregation.

"Friends, I am *so happy* to be here today to share the *truth* with you about God's love and justice."

"Praise God," the congregation said.

"Most of you don't know that I am Reverend Peoples's stepson, Rex. I have written a very special poem for you today that speaks to the Reverend's message of the Fine Line and our power to choose. How we don't have to be afraid when we are aligned with the true love of God. This poem is in honor of my mother…"

"Praise God," the congregation said.

Fear Sticks to Me

A big black, heavy cast iron pan is popping
with bacon fat, next to my smoking man,
cocked like a mannequin at a wobbly, wooden table.
Thick, lively smoke is bellowing around him and I say,
"You know that shit is gonna kill you and it's trashy too!"

He looks at me languidly, adjusting his dingy,
once white, undershirt, and seems oddly
compelled not to slap me, in his usual
"try-to-control-my-shit" manner…
Instead he surprises me by saying, "Baby, I thought
God don't make mistakes, and he don't make trash?"

LANE ROCKFORD ORSAK

"Oh you are one slick business, Mr. Peoples,"
I say, trying to act like his very presence
isn't burning me like the bacon fat landing
on my arm like hot dancing needles.

Bob Peoples just looked down and laughed that same
Dumb-ass chuckle that makes him feel free
from any emotional responsibility, for me,
and then says, "Oh, you are tough my Sista, you are tough…"
smacking his lips together and staring, real hard, at my bacon.
Who ever knew that bourbon, bacon, and eggs could make
someone a dinner? I swear Bob Peoples musta paid
for half them wooden barrels over there in Kentucky,
drinking his every Friday night bourbon, talking about how
he "done-worked-hard and deserved a reward…"

At first, I thought Mr. Peoples was cute, you know — different.
I liked that. I liked men that were different.
I didn't know that up under all that muscle, bourbon,
and "manly Preacher bullshit," was a scared-to-death
little prison boy, trying to play me like a beat-up toy.
I use to tell him, "Baby, I know you been sent to me by God,"
and now, I say, "God damn it, Bob Peoples… if you don't get
your drunk ass off my couch, I will kill you in your sleep!"

The children start crying, he starts screaming and
telling me how lucky I am, cause no other fool would want me.
Then he passes out, and things change.
Fear sticks to me like hot grease, and keeps me far
from anything that could ever make me happy.

In my dreams, I escape like a pissed-off panther
and can't nobody fuck with me. I am large and strong.
I snap him off the couch by the neck and drag him

*outside to the trash can and stuff his good-for-nothing ass
in it, and slam the lid closed, yelling, just like he be yelling,
"Oh yes he do, Bob Peoples, God do make trash,
but he don't live up in my house, no more!"*

When Rex finished the poem, Bob Peoples walked toward him, aggressively.

"You walk one more inch toward me and I will finish you right here." His stepfather stopped dead in his tracks. The congregation was stunned into silence.

"If you ever show your abusive, cheating, criminal face at my mother's house again,

I will have you arrested for fraud, theft, and for stealing *these good people's* money and faith—now, *get the fuck* out of *my* church!"

"Praise God," the congregation said.

Overcoming Coming

• • • • • • •

WE ALL KNEW it was inevitable; it was only a question of *when* Halo and Vanessa had to talk about what happened that night after the RoosterCock. Keegan observed that they had been avoiding one another, as he said, "like cock and robber." Halo's usual masculine vibrato had been eclipsed lately by a squeaky pubescence. And Vanessa's vivacious Brooklyn sass and brass was definitely on mute. For the first time at the Ho Gym, we had a morale problem. Something had to give, and finally that day arrived.

Rex and I were at the front desk, acting silly as usual. Vanessa came over, and stood there looking pathetic as she watched Halo teach a boot-camp class.

"You know, while that boy ain't got much personality, one must admit, he is a *manly* chisel of rock, if you know what I mean!"

"Oh, so you think he is a Big Mac and a bag of fries," I offered.

"Oh, Miss Jackie, I *just know* he has a double meat patty."

"Hate to disappoint you two, but it's more like a Junior Whopper!" Vanessa said, approaching the front desk.

Moments later, Halo ran over to the counter with a look of horror. "I can hear you guys, and therefore *my class* can hear, *every word* you fools are saying… and if anyone is the 'Junior Whopper' around here, it is you, Vanessa, or should I say 'Van—the Man!'"

And that is when all hell broke loose.

The Brooklyn bombshell blew up. "What the fuck did you just call me? My name is *Vanessa*, and I don't have a dick, for your information. I am *all woman,* or were you too drunk to remember that when we slept together?"

Halo's class seemed thoroughly entertained. He stood motionless and stunned leaning against the front desk, with all five feet, two inches of Vanessa right in his face.

"Of course, you haven't even had the fucking decency to speak to me after the fact, ask me how I'm doing, or inquire how I might be feeling. Is that what they taught you in SEAL training, to attack and fall back... to be dumb and numb? Well, you're not *that numb...* you didn't seem to mind it when I blew you, rolled you over, and put my toy in your foxhole. You seemed to feel something *then!*"

Vanessa made loud, erotic moaning sounds, peppered with the finale, "Oh, baby, fuck me..." just to punctuate her point.

We all braced for Halo's exothermic nuclear reaction.

He walked over to her and stood silently in front of her. He put his arms around her gently, and said, "I am really sorry, Vanessa, I love you." He kissed her for a long time, which caused his class to go ballistic with cheers and applause.

Rex looked at me as if his world was just turned upside down. "Well, if that ain't the strangest fight I have ever witnessed *in my life.* That was stranger than fiction. Child, you can not make that shit up!"

Old Man and The Sea

• • • • • • • • • • •

DAD STILL WENT to Gold's on Tuesdays to work out. I didn't have time to go with him like when I was a kid, but I did meet him afterward for lunch at the Firehouse. It felt great to have him back in my life. It was such a relief to not carry the burden of the past on my shoulders and to be just a loving daughter.

When I arrived, Dad seemed more serious than usual. He didn't even call me his little princess.

"Hey Dad—what's up?"

"Hello, sweetheart. I'm so happy to see you."

"Have you already ordered?"

"Yes, I ordered the usual with extra veggies."

"Yum… What's up with the long face?"

"Fiona left me this morning."

"Wow, that was fast, I didn't even get to meet her! What happened?"

"Oh I don't know, sweetheart, something about how I don't *really* love her, I don't know how to love, or let anyone *in* to love me—the usual chick stuff!"

"How long did you and Fiona date?"

"I guess it was about six months."

"Dad, what is the longest romantic relationship you've had with a woman?"

I didn't ask my Dad to upset him. I wasn't trying to pry into his secret drawer, I just wanted to understand why such a handsome man, with a successful professional career never seemed to be in a relationship for long.

Dad surprised me. He put his face into his big muscular hands and let out a big sigh.

"The truth is, Bar, they never last long."

"Maybe what Fiona said is true. Maybe you do have a problem letting people in to love you. Maybe you share your body and not your heart. The problem is, bodies don't last, Dad."

"What's wrong, darling? I don't want to upset you, sweetheart."

I put my napkin over my face and felt my face heat up with waves of sadness.

"Bar, what is it, honey?"

"Mom has cancer."

"Oh my God. What kind?"

"Breast cancer."

"Who is taking care of her? I train one of the best oncologists in the city and I'll call him after our lunch."

"Dad, wait. She is going to be OK. She has breast cancer and they've caught it in time. It just makes me realize how precious our lives are and what is important. Wow, I was trying to cheer you up and look at me, I am a mess…"

"You sure she is gonna be OK, sweetheart?"

"Yeah, Dad, just thought you should know."

I excused myself to the ladies' room and the television in the bar happened to be on with the local news. I heard the announcer say that fishermen found an older, homeless man off the Santa Monica Pier this morning. The police had not identified the man, but one local surfer said he was known as "Plato," and he was thought to reside in Venice Beach.

My heart ached with the news. I called Maxi, and he was *really* upset. He asked me to come to the gym. Plato had left a note and he needed me to read it to him.

I told Dad the news and he drove me to the gym.

"I'm sorry to hear about your friend, Bar. Call me if you need anything."

"Thanks, Dad, just your love."

"You always have that, kid!"

Inside the gym, Maxi was back in Plato's apartment. It was empty. Plato had cleaned and cleared away anything that he had collected over the last year. On the old wooden table was a note. Maxi was seated, with his hand barely holding his forehead.

When I walked in, he asked seriously, "Bar, did I do this to Plato? Did I cause this? Was there something I should have done? I am so unhappy."

I gave him a big hug. "Of course you didn't. He loved you. He loved all of us."

After several minutes of silence, I summoned the courage to pick up the note. It was definitely Plato's handwriting, clear and beautifully printed.

Maxi My Friend –

Thank you for your beautiful, boundless energy and kind affection. You helped facilitate something truly fabulous for me, and the kids.

I hope you won't mind, but I donated your generous financial gift to create a scholarship fund for young, aspiring artists. I have named it SAMO (Seek Art More Often). The Director will contact you soon. Please, join the Board in my absence.

I visited a physician. It seems that I am not well. He gave me little time to live. I am tired, my friend, so very tired.

I leave for you the last ounce of love in my being to say thank you.

Your loyal friend,
Plato

P.S. Please kiss my darling Barbella on the forehead for me. She is such a fine girl. The finest.

Mom acted like her chemo treatments were a piece of cake, as if her body was an automobile and she would simply take it into the shop—Cancer Lube—and they would give her a quick treatment and she would be good as new. Tonya gave me the real scoop. Even though Mom stayed strong for the world, at home she would break down in her studio when the chemo was really tough on her. Her oncologist wanted to reduce the size of the tumor with chemo before removing her breasts. It was shocking to see my mom, still so young, so fit and healthy, with cancer. She spent her entire life watching what she put into her body and now they were essentially putting nuclear energy into her in hope of killing the tumor's growth. I felt so angry, and under that, afraid.

The airline gave her a medical leave of absence, but she already confided in me that she wanted to retire. Her jewelry business was going well and she hoped that with the money from Maxi, maybe she and I could partner on a small boutique in Santa Monica. I loved the idea and was happy to do it. Besides, the real-estate prices in Venice were going nuts. Everything was so expensive. Especially since Giggle came to Venice.

When it was time for her big surgery, she told me that they would have to reconstruct her nipples after they removed her breasts. She *hated* that idea. She was upset for over a week and finally she told me that she had figured out how to make it OK. "Stars," she said. "I am going to have stars tattooed on my breasts, instead of faux nipples. Hell, I'll wear my own two-star constellation!"

Tonya did such an amazing job caring for Mom after her surgery. But after Mom had recovered well enough to move around, Tonya decided to return to England. It was clear to her that even though she loved training with all of her heart, body, and soul, she simply would never be "big enough" to win an international competition.

Tonya told me that Dad had been coming around lately, and trying to help out. He never mentioned it to me, nor did Mom.

Apparently, he took great pride in preparing meals for her, which he called "Renzo's Super Healer Cuisine." He tried to entertain her with stories about his bodybuilding celebrity clients and the old gang. Before he left her condo, he would say, "Babe, Venice is a better place with you in it."

Last I heard, Tonya had become something of an Internet superstar. It seems that her enlarged clitoris, due to her massive steroid use, was now the size of a baby boy's penis, and it had given her a unique place in the porn industry. Apparently, she was capturing enough kinky fans to make a nice living doing a *live* Internet show, including face time posing, a raucous blog, and merchandise. The most exciting item was an anatomically correct, life-size plastic "Tonya Doll."

Maxi Ho Gym on Steroids

• • • • • • • • • • • •

I WAS LEARNING so much about humanity. My clients were from every age group and background. I seemed to attract the young men that wanted more than anything in life to feel like a "man." Which, to them, meant to get "shredded," to be able to go home and flex that bicep in the mirror, to tighten their abs and imagine getting that hot bombie. Or the middle-aged man who struggled with his midsection. They would spent most of the session telling me about what they used to be able to do and how different it was now. Whatever the reality of the client's fitness goals, the overarching truth is that they were all fleeting relationships, and they began to feel increasingly hollow.

Over the next six months, Maxi almost never visited the temporary gym up the street, and he absolutely forbade any of us to see the new gym. He told me, "Bar, you are my number one Manager Boss Lady. You are now a true *pali pali* girl!"

I loved our temporary gym at 78 Market Street. It was in a historic redbrick building, which at first reminded me of the Main at Miss Palmer's School. It had more room than the old gym and much higher ceilings. When I went by the old gym, now under full construction, I could hear Maxi cursing in Korean at the crews. With the mega attention brought on by the sale of the Basquiat painting discovery, all the publicity about Maxi's life story and his amazing father, and all the lives he touched in Venice, folks were begging to join the gym. We had to hire new trainers, offer more classes, stay open later, and bring three new "massage ladies" from Hooker Hill.

Every week, I watched our old rundown gym grow taller, more modern, and more interesting. Maxi brought a hip young architect from Seoul to do the design work. He insisted that the building orientation change, to face the Pacific Ocean, and demanded that Maxi buy the parking lot next door to allow for a more dramatic entrance. The building was stunningly modern, but employed elements that paid tribute to ancient Korean monuments. At the base of the building, on the ground floor, he used large slick black stones that gave it a solid feeling and a nod to ancient Korean castles. The next layer was red-orange colored stucco. The second floor was demarcated with marigold-colored stucco. I realized that all the surface colors could be found in the palette of Basquiat's painting, "Art Opening 1982." The third floor was mind-bendingly cool. He built a huge terrace that curved toward the beach in a crescent shape.

Across the entire upper floor were private skyboxes jutting out of the building for personal ocean-view workouts. The window design was in the shape of a large H. On either side of this level were enormous sculptural steel barbells that could be seen for miles. The pièce de résistance was the rooftop terrace, which featured a covered Juicy Café + Bar, a running track, and a stainless-steel lap pool. On the Market Street side of the building were two sets of beautiful glass elevators that went to every floor. On the Zephyr Court side of the building, a huge rock-climbing wall was installed so at any point of the day you could see people climbing up the building.

The new gym was causing quite a stir. The press called it "One Ho-lacious new gym." One simply couldn't visit Venice Beach and not see the new muscle monument from the Boardwalk. It was as if the architecture commanded the viewer to enter and exercise. It was probably the largest and coolest-looking gym in the world.

Maxi was very hush-hush about the interior design, but he had crews working almost around the clock. He told me that he was going to have a huge opening party. He was hiring a well-known Hollywood publicist and wanted it to be the party of the year.

We were all starting to freak out. It was like Maxi had gone mad. In fact, Rex now referred to him at "Mad Maxi!"

I was so busy at work that Apti and I had little time to spend together. I started worrying that we might be growing apart. He was enrolled at UCLA and always seemed to be studying. Also, his dad returned from Europe and expected him to spend more time at home, especially when he learned about his American girlfriend and the Giggle incident. But soon his dad realized that I was not just an In-N-Out burger to his son and he was super nice to me. I still felt Apti's presence as I moved through time and space. It was hard to explain, but there was simply never a moment in my life that I didn't want to be around him. I wanted to touch him, care about him—I was truly in love with him.

Apti always said stupid things like, "I'm sure you will find some hot sexy Hollywood actor and run off to shoot a film in Italy." As absurd as it felt to me, somehow in his mind it could happen, a real possibility. I think that for people who prematurely lost their childhood innocence, it was a lifelong challenge to trust that life could be lovely, and not live in constant fear of the worst that could happen.

It made me think of my clients with body dysmorphia, the ones who constantly ask me, "Do I look fat?" Their greatest fear becomes their default feeling. I understood this. Every time I felt stressed, fearful, or uncertain I wanted to pop candy corns in my mouth. The difference now is that I acknowledge the desire, have learned to love myself, and choose not to do it.

Finally, the big day arrived for all of us to see our new gym. Max waited until the cleaning crews had finished and everyone on staff could make it. Maxi had it catered for us and turned it into what he called a "Staff Boom Boom Party." First, he took us all to the front of the building. It was a cool evening and dark, and we all stood like little kids and held hands as we waited for the lights to go up. Maxi gave a brief speech thanking us for our dedication and hoped that the new gym would give us plenty of "Boom Boom Happy Disco" and then said, "Hit it!"

The building lights were turned on and we all had the same reaction: "Oh, wow! Incredible!" The lights illuminated the big barbell on top of the building. And over the entrance, in huge steel channel letters across the front, glowing in hot neon, read SAMO HO GYM. We all applauded wildly. Many of the original gang started crying. It was amazing.

Below, in smaller steel letters, read, IT'S DEFINITELY WORTH MORE THAN ¥200.

Inside, the first thing I experienced was the deep bass beat of the incredible sound system. It made me feel like I was floating, but in an exciting way with hip electronic fusion music. A beautiful young Korean girl, wearing all black except for a t-shirt that had SAMO in red-orange letters and HO in white on the front, bowed and welcomed me. She offered me a personal sound system that allowed me to listen to the house mix, which was generated by a live DJ in the booth high above the gym floor. Or I could select from more than forty custom playlists in every musical genre. The front desk was covered with smooth, shining iridescent mother-of-pearl shell and curved in an organic shape. Tall panels of thick glass separated the space, allowing one to see into the gym's high ceilings, the gorgeous state-of-the-art workout equipment, and the various staging areas. Moroccan red curved walls led me into the main space, and to the right was a gift shop that Maxi named PLATO'S RETREAT.

This was not the usual gym shop filled with Speedos, t-shirts, shorts, and white socks for members that forgot workout clothes. This was a Korean-pop gift shop. The first thing I noticed was the sex-toy vending machine, named Green Love, with crazy anime figures on the packaging, offering a wild variety items with wacky names like Man S, Double Clitoris Anal Toy, or Flexible Vibrator Rabbit Gold, Rotation Toy. There was an entire wall of built-in merchandise (bags, aprons, shorts, etc.) and shelves with Samo Ho t-shirts. Some had sayings on the front like, Dogtown Diva, Ho Rida, Cardio Ho, Downward Dog Ho, and seasonal selections like HO HO HO!

There were exclusive SAMO HO music mixes, including all the hottest and latest K-Pop stars. Not to mention the myriad of gifts, like the Korean Poo Stationery set. There were wildly bold and colorful socks with K-pop stars, owls, monkeys, and pandas. A beauty line with essence facemasks designed to fit over your face, with aromas like pearl extract, red ginseng and green tea. I think that Plato was rolling over in his grave, with the idea that a kitschy gift shop was named in his honor.

I was standing next to Rex. He smirked. "Little Jackie, this place is clearly for 'bawdy builders.'"

I was struck by the majesty of the main gym room. It felt Olympic. The focal point was a massive stage for performances, contests, or events that had steel catwalks going on either side, leading to posing stands. Maxi hired beautiful, shredded bodybuilders, both men and women, to slowly pose. They created an immediate mood of physical beauty. I had grown up in a bodybuilder gym, but this was something different. The walls were jet black, with huge mirrors on two walls. The deadweight area was amazing. Maxi had hired "Plate Heads" to help the members by getting barbells, adding weights to the machines, serving them spring water, or giving a hand with spotting as needed.

The group fitness rooms were stellar, including the pole-dancing studio. And the yoga studio had authentic Japanese *tatami* mats and a water wall. The entire black stone wall had water gently flowing down into a catch basin, creating a lovely sense of tranquility. The Parkour Skate Training Room was custom-designed by Apti to give clients the ultimate in opportunity to run, jump, and flip, including a massive subterranean in-ground bowl for skating. Maxi also built an Observation Room, so tourists could pay to watch folks train, and of course enjoy a delicious smoothie or cocktail from the third-floor Juicy Bar + Café.

The second-floor spa area was Zen personified. You entered a Transformation Room, where guests would change into soft cotton Japanese *yukata* (cotton robes) and a solemn attendant washed your feet in warm rosemary and lavender oils. Another attendant would guide you to the appropriate part of the spa: skin care, massage, or total relaxation in a "Maxi Ho Selfie Tube" which featured guided mediation tapes, instrumental relaxation music, or the Maxi Ho Boom Boom channel. *Don't ask!*

Maxi called the third floor "Skybox Training." Across the entire expanse, he built private training spaces that looked out onto the Pacific Ocean and led to a private balcony. There, after your workout, your lunch, breakfast, or dinner, you could be served as you relaxed with a cool ocean breeze.

At the roof terrace, I was flabbergasted by the cool factor. The Juicy Bar + Café was a knockout with a stellar ocean view. Maxi brought in a super-fresh chef from Mexico who specialized in healthy, organic, sexy Asian-Latin American fusion cuisine. The bar served health-conscious cocktails. And of course, Maxi had a line of soju (Korean sake) specialty drinks: Pink Apple Soju, a Citrus-Soju Collins, a Mango Sour Soju, and my favorite, a Soju & Blueberry Shrub cocktail. Maxi planned on keeping the roof terrace open until two a.m. to capture the late-night beach bar trade.

The night was magical. We all laughed, ate, drank, explored and ultimately ended up watching the stars and talking about crazy clients, the early days of the gym, and the special friend that we lost along the way. It was the first time after Plato's death that we were all able to be together. We never really had a chance to have a funeral for Plato, or any kind of spiritual service. He probably would he have hated a traditional funeral.

As we always did, we looked to Rex to lead us in honoring our friend.

"Lord, we gather as friends, in a spirit of love and gratitude, to honor our departed friend and loved one, Plato. First, I would like to acknowledge that never in the history of any business establishment on Earth has there ever been an older, thinner, and less muscular person in charge of 'security.' Thank you, Lord, that our Plato didn't have to wrangle with any bad folks on the job!

"The irony, of course is that he was in the truest sense our greatest security and strength. Through his own life's tremendous personal loss and pain, he was able to give abundance and joy to others. He instinctually felt the feelings of those in his presence and made every effort to extend that compassion and love.

"Plato saw my struggles, fears, and insecurities as an aspiring poet and writer. It was as if he could read my interior world and when I was feeling the most unsure, he would smile that warm, loving, gaze and playfully remind me of what my grandmother Petite Savoie use to tell us, 'Baby, God don't make mistakes, and he don't make trash.' If I was really feeling low, he might quote the Dalai Lama: *'The planet doesn't need more successful people. The planet desperately needs more peacemakers, healers, restorers, storytellers and lovers of all kinds.'*"

Rex began to cry and found it hard to continue. Halo walked over and put his arms around Rex and spoke.

"Some time ago, a little girl came to our gym named Nancy. Her dad was an ex-military officer and told her daily that she was fat, disgusting, and a disgrace to their family. After our first session, she ran into the restroom and wouldn't come out. What I didn't know is that Plato had a key, and went in to speak to her. I don't know what he said, but he came to find me, and let me know about how fragile and hurt she was. I panicked. I didn't know how to deal with fragile. I was trained to find weakness and use it to my advantage against an enemy—to kill them—not nurture them.

"Plato saw the panic in my eyes. At first, I told him I couldn't do it, you guys would have to find another trainer better suited for the task. He smiled with his kind and loving eyes deeply into mine and said, 'Son, God has put her in your path to reverse the karma of killing. Now you must devote yourself to a path of compassion and loving. This little girl needs your encouragement, and you can give her that. It is within you!' My greatest accomplishment at the gym, besides finding my love Vanessa, was to watch that little girl grow, to become strong, joyous, and find her own inner beauty. Thank you, Plato."

Halo stood at attention and snapped a salute of honor and respect. Vanessa sweetly looked at everyone with tears streaming down her face. "I can't talk right now. I just want to say I will miss you, Plato!"

Apti just smiled through his tears.

"I am grateful for you all and will miss Plato," Apti said. "He met me when I arrived in Venice. Actually, it was Plato that caught me stealing a loaf of bread from Mr. Ho. He stopped me as I left and he noticed the big bulge of bread under my shirt. He smiled kindly and said, 'Where is the dignity in stealing from another?' He extended his long arm toward me and gave me a five-dollar bill and said, 'You are stealing Mr. Ho's property, but more disturbing is the fact that you are truly robbing your own dignity. Go pay the man for his bread.'

"Once inside, Mr. Ho realized what had happened and gave me an afterschool job at the grocery. If it weren't for Plato and Mr. Ho, I don't know what would have happened.

"After I began working here at the gym, Plato and I spent many hours talking. He helped me with my incalculable amount of pain of losing my mother and sister, and my fear to love with all of my heart."

Apti looked over at me and couldn't continue. I put my arm around him.

Maxi stood up. "Time for my Plato Boom Boom speech — ne!

"This will be difficult to tell you. Plato has been rocking in front of my father's store for many years. My father also had much loss in his life back in Korea during the war. He lost his family, village, and his true love, my mother, back in Seoul. He came to America to find a new life, to prosper, to live an American dream of prosperity. There were many hardships and struggles.

"Before he died, he told me, 'Son, the only thing that will matter to you when you are an old man, is that you have worked hard to become rich, not rich in gold or silk, rich in soul. Soul is woven slowly, from many years of loving, in the face of the pain in this world.'

"My father cared for Plato when he was too fragile to care for himself. That is why he wouldn't leave this building. The reason that Plato couldn't leave this place before is because of his love for all of you. He had to plant his love in your hearts so you could all take this out into the world and plant more seeds."

I tried my best to share some personal thoughts.

"I don't mean to sound cliché, but the love of Mr. Ho, Maxi, and Plato have brought tremendous good to a lot of people's lives. It can sometimes be hard to recognize these efforts when our lives are so wrapped up in activities. The greatest thing that Plato taught me is that love can be found in the most unlikely of places, in a grocery store, in a gym, or on the street from a homeless person. Plato understood my fears and insecurities and gave me his love. I will really miss him."

Rex stood and everyone joined him holding hands. "Let us close this circle of love with a final prayer. Heavenly Father, we thank you for this safe space to share our feelings and love and we ask that you hold Plato in our hearts forever…"

Everyone said, "Amen." And in a strange moment of spontaneity, Rex ran everyone toward the pool, and screamed, "For Plato!" and we all jumped in the water simultaneously, crying, laughing, and splashing.

Full Circle

· · · · · · · · · ·

WELL, AS ONE would expect, the Grand Opening Party for Samo Ho Gym was a smashing success. The place was crawling with stars, famous bodybuilders—and, yes, his majesty of muscle, "the Austrian Oak," made an appearance. I even saw Apti speaking Russian to Serge Brantov from Giggle.

At some point later in the evening after we were all very illuminated on Soju Slings, Rex and a famous Ukrainian fashion model climbed up on the concrete wall at the pool, near naked, and did synchronized swan dives. Mad Maxi hired gorgeous topless dancers/models to work the posing stages, to pass drinks and hors d'oeuvres. He hired the British artist Seal to perform live at the event. It felt particularly apropos when he sang his hit song, "Crazy."

After rescuing Rex from nearly drowning in the arms of Oksana Jovovich, I decided to go down and find Maxi. As I made my way through the crowds of "beautiful people," I was stopped in my tracks when the crowd parted and directly in front of me was a dashing looking man laughing with another couple and poised on his arm was a stunning woman with long curly blonde hair laughing and loudly pronouncing, "Oh quite, my dear!"

Clarissa Westwick, my old roommate at Miss Palmer's School.

At first, I was stunned and found it hard to speak. It was like I was back at school. I wanted to run to our dorm bathroom and purge. I felt the cold tile floors on my bare feet, the freezing winter air sneaking past our window.

Clarissa didn't see me at first. She was still so perfect—radiant. Slowly my feelings changed from wonderment to tightness in my stomach and I remembered wanting to strangle her for throwing me under the bus. *Why was she here? Should I rip her fucking hair out?*

I decided to avoid her and leave the party. As I tried to slip past, Maxi, now drunk, screamed, "Barbella—I love you big Boom Boom!"

Clarissa turned instantly and spotted me. She flashed her huge mischievous smile at me and moved toward me. I felt panicked. *What would I say to her? You lying little bitch, how could you get me kicked out of school?*

"Bar Darling, I am so happy to see you!"

"Wow!" was all I could say. "How did you know I was here?"

"I am in town visiting my friend Rupert Lord and your gym has been in the media everywhere. I saw an article in the *Los Angeles Times* about the whole affair and Rupert suggested we come tonight. I jumped at the chance, so hoping that we would meet. I am *happy to see you.*"

"Clarissa, honestly, for me *it's not happy*. I just keep remembering what Kitty and Bunny said to me in Miss Wescott's office before I left."

"Kitty and Bunny? What did those persnickety little prats tell you?"

"About how you were kissing Brook in the Main restroom and how you encountered Miss Wescott after the performance, and told her about where she could find me…"

"Actually darling, Brook and I found Kitty and Bunny in the bathroom kissing and we chased them out. They must have run off and told Miss Wescott."

"You are lying. Look at me, and tell me the truth."

Clarissa stopped talking. She stood silently staring into my eyes. The booming techno pop made our words feel grotesque and hollow. Her denying telling me the truth felt ugly and painful.

I was so angry that tears began to well in my eyes and Clarissa looked down and turned her head. We were in a deadlock. The energy around us felt like sumo wrestlers locked in impasse—both pushing with equal determination for victory. Finally, it came.

"I did admit to Miss Wescott, after we got caught, that I helped you nail Kate Cunningham, and why. I told her *everything* that they had done to us. As a so-called accomplice, and my father's enormous financial contribution to construct the new Westwick Theatre, I was simply put on probation. I tried my best to dissuade Miss Wescott from expelling you, darling, but I am afraid Kitty and Bunny's fathers are on the Board."

"That all sounds so *tidy* Clarissa. You know damn well that you told Miss Wescott on the day of the Wishing on the Ring Ceremony and you told her everything to save yourself from being expelled—at my expense.

Clarissa lifted her head and looked directly into my eyes. She stared blankly for the longest time.

"Bar Darling. I *couldn't* face going home. You have no idea what that would have meant to my family, to my future—it would have been a bloody disaster."

"So throwing me under the bus, was not a fucking disaster *for me*? It didn't affect my family, my future?"

Clarissa soon had tears streaming down her perfect cheeks. Inexplicably, seeing her pain, her vulnerability, caused my anger to lift from my body and I just stood before her observing her and I realized that Clarissa was not as strong and free as she worked so hard to portray to the world… she was trapped, like any girl at Miss Palmer's. She loved to try on exciting ideas of freedom and have "adventures," but she was utterly terrified to be excluded from the security of her family, social position, and financial future. She knew it and I knew it, but this would never be discussed.

"Clarissa, you have no idea how much I needed to see you again."

"Bar Darling, I do hope you can forgive me. The fact that I adore you is not a lie. That I truly value you, and want us to be friends, does live in the deepest part of my heart. You are truly the best thing that happened for me at Miss P's, and in some kind of divine intervention sort of way, I see that you are exactly where you belong and that you are so much happier."

"I am, Clarissa, *more than I can say*, I am."

Strangely, in that precise moment, hearing myself say that I was happy, was the first time I had acknowledged happiness in years and I understood how sad, truly sad, Clarissa's situation was for her. In recognizing this, I found a deeper sense of appreciation for my own freedom — the courage to forge my own life — and I was able to forgive her, and let in some love for myself.

Strong Enough To Be My Man

• • • • • • • • • • • • • •

SAMO HO GYM was on the A-list of Hollywood must-be-seen locales for the first year. After we re-opened it was always packed, bringing paparazzi, police, madness, and mayhem. Now, four years later, it is mostly tourists. The gym has changed. Our core group of trainers gradually moved in different directions. The new trainers at the gym were all slick and impressive in their knowledge and skills, but I didn't feel connected to them as I did with the old gang. I started feeling like it was time to maybe move on.

I had given Maxi all of my love, time, and energy. The gym was wildly successful. Money would never be a problem for him. I was so pleased for his success, but I was growing ever more restless. I couldn't pretend to care about another person's abs, or their desire to be ripped. I didn't want to see another scrawny Chinese student with bird legs and scrawny arms, the son of a captain of the booming construction industry in China building skyscraper cities in two weeks, pulling up in his pimped-out $400,000 Lamborghini at the front door. I needed something else.

Franco and Raquel moved to Manhattan—actually Brooklyn—to work at his old "no judgment" gym in Chelsea. His former client, Peter Paxton, is now a *big deal* in the NYC movie scene, and has re-hired Franco to "torture him," as he calls it. Raquel is training the NYC University girls' volleyball team and reports that "clam slamming" has not yet made it to the city.

Vanessa and Halo flew to Las Vegas and got married. Vanessa insisted they both dress as Elvis Presley, and wanted to wear a strap-on, in honor of the first evening together. Their reception party was held at the RoosterCock and involved ridiculous amounts of "Wise Men" shots and dancing. "Prince Albert" was nowhere to be seen. Vanessa soon opened her own yoga studio in West Hollywood. She claims her clients are the strangest people on earth, all doing downward dogs when they shouldn't. Halo got a small role in a hit television series about covert ops in the Middle East. They seemed really happy.

After he chased Bob Peoples off, Rex was able to rent the church to a real reverend, find a cute bungalow for his mom, and concentrate on his passion for theater and writing. He was producing his own plays and getting a great deal of attention from critics who hailed him as a "bright light in theater, and a jubilant force to be reckoned with…"

My favorite client, Keegan, still sends me an occasional note or sonnet. I'll always be grateful for him helping Apti. He swears that it wasn't him, but recently someone shut down Giggle in a very similar fashion. I think he is working in San Francisco on some kind of top-secret digital global security firewall. In his last message he said it was as big as the American "Star Wars" program, but he couldn't talk about it.

Hellena, our resident British eccentric, moved back to her family's estate in Oxfordshire, England. I understand that she wanted her American-born son to learn to brew a "proper" cup of tea. I was amused to learn from Rex—whom she adored—that she had created an exotic series of children's fantasy books. Apparently, the story takes place in the Cotswolds at a large manor home, near six canals, called "Mrs. Slocombe's Pussy."

After only three years, Apti graduated from UCLA with a double degree in global marketing and computer technology. It seems that he doesn't dislike Serge Brantov as much as he previously thought, and is now working in Giggle's global marketing department. When I asked him about his "conscience," he responded, "Who am I to argue with God?"

Soon after I decided to leave the gym, Apti and I did a really long run along the ocean. After we returned to my apartment, he said, "You know, Bar... I love this place, but I think maybe we should think more about our own future living arrangements. At the rate the real-estate prices are climbing, we will not be able to afford our own house in Venice. And now that I am out of school and working, there is something I have been meaning to ask you."

I just stared at him blankly as my stomach tightened.

He gently touched my face and kissed my lips, and smiled a smile that I felt down to my toes. "Please, my lovely friend, my little Platypus, will you marry me?"

Of course, I said yes.

We were married immediately and had the reception on the roof terrace at the gym. Maxi insisted on paying for everything, saying, "I will give you a Boom Boom wedding party you will never forget!" He also paid for everyone to fly home to Venice for the wedding. Mom invited Tonya to come from England, and I must say, she looked surprisingly feminine in her short black dress. Well, except for her huge biceps. Just to be funny fools, both Rex and Halo wore dresses to my wedding, of course Halo's ensemble included combat boots, and Vanessa and Keegan came in matching pink tuxedos. Maxi paid for a helicopter to fly over the roof terrace and deliver Apti, who came down on a long ladder in his red parkour shoes, skate shorts with the peace signs, a white t-shirt with a bowtie and a black tux jacket.

Mom insisted on being the flower girl and Dad seemed really proud to walk me down the aisle. And if you ask me, they are sweet on each other again.

It was hard for me not to cry the entire celebration. It wasn't a wedding that anyone from Miss Palmer's School would have approved of, even though Clarissa and Rupert Lord attended, but I was really happy.

For our honeymoon, Sophie and Claude invited us to vacation at Claude's ranch in French New Caledonia. It was gorgeous. And yes, I did see a real platypus in the wild. *What was I thinking?*

After we returned to our lives in Venice, I had another huge surprise for Apti. We had our own little Parkour Princess waiting to join us. Apti freaked out with excitement. Mom was amazing and helped me every step of the way during my pregnancy. Now that Olivia is with us, besides being a little germ magnet, she is the most precious thing I have ever seen, and Apti and I are "Maxi Mad" in love with her.

"Olivia Sandrine Murid, do you know your precious little body has more than six hundred and fifty muscles?" Apti placed our daughter's soft, feverish head onto his strong, lean chest.

In my exhausted state, I said, "Darling, just let her sleep. What will you be doing next, teaching her parkour in her crib? That's all we need, is to have our sweet baby kicking in her sleep, with a cast on, in the crib." I started laughing at my own silly impromptu alliteration and then blurted out, "Oh my God, she's gonna need a custom skateboard by time she's two!"

Apti gently looked into my eyes. "Sorry, darling. I'm just so in love with our beautiful daughter!"

Even though I was deliriously tired, I could feel precisely what it is that allows love to flow from one human heart to another—and I began to cry from the extraordinary amount that I felt for my lovely husband and my precious little daughter, Olivia.

Epilogue

NOW THAT I am much older, and Olivia is preparing to go off to school, I went through her things to help her pack. I found an old shoebox filled with ancient childhood treasures. On the bottom was a tiny bead bracelet. It was the first piece of jewelry I made for her when Mom and I opened the shop in Santa Monica. It said, simply, BOOM BOOM. Memories flooded my mind about Maxi, the gym, the gang, and who I was at that time in my life.

Now I realized something important that Plato once told me, something I couldn't fully understand at the time. He said:

"Darling girl, this world will demand that you play the game. It will taunt and tease you with desires, give you moments of amazement and splendor and then push your face down to the floor in fear. But, at the end, you will look back and realize that it is often when you are the most uncertain on your path, when you live truly in the moment and feel your feelings, perhaps even when you feel completely lost, that you are in fact the most alive, and found. And the people you share your true feelings with, regardless of their appearance, sexual orientation, religious preference, or financial position, those who truly accept you — as you are — are a true gift."

What he was trying to teach me was that although I worked at a struggling gym, so unsure of my future and myself, I was in a beautiful circumstance that was filled with acceptance, love, hope, energy, care, and laughter. That I — we — the gang — was being given a precious gift. A brief moment in time of tremendous grace and it was not to be taken for granted.

How did I ever get so lucky? Thank you, God. Thank you.

• • •

About the author

• •

LANE ROCKFORD ORSAK began his creative life in children's theater, with a mother who was the first woman on television for ABC in Houston, Texas (*Kitirik*, 1954–1971). He studied acting and the Liberal Arts at Lon Morris College and graduated from the University of Texas, where he danced two seasons in the Austin Ballet Theatre.

His musical *Mr. Hanks* was accepted to audition at the prestigious BMI Lehman Engel Musical Theater Workshop in New York City, and his young adult *Keiko the Fairy* book series was accepted by the president of Paramount Pictures Animation in Los Angeles for consideration.

He founded Creative Marketing Consultants in 2000, which provides advertising, design, and marketing services in Austin, Texas. For more information visit:

www.laneorsak.com